The African
Poetry and Drama

The African Poetry and Drama

edited by

SHYAM S. AGARWALLA

PRESTIGE

Published by

PRESTIGE BOOKS

3/28, East Patel Nagar

New Delhi 110 008

2000

ISBN: 81-7551-070-6

Composed by Vivek Mathur, Delhi 110 006 Ph., 3981867

Printed by Dhawan Industries Offset, New Delhi 110 028

Contents

African Drama

Contributors

SHYAM S. AGARWALLA	Dr. Ram Manohar Lohia College Ranchi
CURWEN BEST	University of the West Indies Bridgetown, Barbados
NEERJA JAYAL CHAND	R.L.A. College University of Delhi
A.P. DANI	Fergusson College Pune
PAUL O IHEAKARAM	Alvan Ikoku College of Ed. Owerri, Imo State, Nigeria
TABAN LO LIYONG	University of Venda Thohoyandou, South Africa
BASAVARAJ S. NAIKAR	Karnatak University Dharwad
M. PUSHPA	Bharati Women's College Madras
K. VENKATA REDDY	S.K. University Anantapur
SARBANI SEN	University of Poona Pune
S. SREERAMULU	V.R.S. Degree College Veerapunayunipalli, Cuddapah
DEREK WRIGHT	University of Queensland Brisbane, Queensland

The African Literature: An Introduction

SHYAM S. AGARWALLA

Africa lies right across the equator, and spreads a much greater proportion of its surface between the tropics than any other continent. With Europe and Asia, it forms the largest continuous land surface of the globe; but its coasts are far less indented than theirs, and it is altogether more uniform and self-contained. Another characteristic is that while to the north and west, deserts and low coastal plains prevail, south and east of the basins of the Congo and the upper Nile have vast tablelands behind the littoral, with an average height of some 3,500 feet above sea level.

Below the mountain ranges, steppes and fertile littoral of the northern shores of Africa, there stretches the Sahara, the greatest of deserts, forming with the Libyan and Arabian deserts a broad belt of inhospitable sands that runs eastward from the Atlantic to the Persian Gulf and the Euphrates valley. This desert barrier divides the rest of the continent from its northern coastlands far more effectually than the Mediterranean separates Africa from Europe. W. Basil Worsfold says: "it [Africa] was a land of surprises . . . of the fifteenth and sixteenth centuries. . . . The Christian powers, in their absorption in the fierce contest of the Crescent and the Cross, stifled an African civilization which was the equal of their own, labelled the whole interior of the continent as unknown and unknowable, and then three centuries later set themselves laboriously to illuminate the dark continent whose chief civilization they had themselves extinguished, and to discover and evangelise the very countries they had themselves brought to an end." The Empire of the Two Shores, which in its zenith ruled from the Pyrenees to the Senegal, created with it the splendid Arabic-Berber civilization under which from the tenth to the sixteenth century first Moslem Spain, and later Moslem North Africa, held centres of learning and enlightenment more advanced in scientific knowledge than any that could be found in Christendom. In the books of es-Sadi (1596-1656), an African historian, one finds, the flight of the learned and wealthy classes from Timbuktu on the approach of Souni Ali's army in 1468, and also comments on the educational value of 'games' for school children to much better effect than the German philosopher Schiller. One finds no scope for doubt about the greatness of the civilization of Timbuktu in the fifteenth and sixteenth centuries.

Another important aspect of the civilization of Africa is concerned with the geographical or racial origin of the peoples called 'Bantu.' The superiority of the Bantu in comparison with the Negro is shown by the richness of their language and political organization. They have an adequate language, and, while there is no written literature, the traditions of the tribes are preserved by oral narrative and folk-lore. They have a simple, but fully developed, tribal system of government, with a body of customary law, tribunals of justice and a system of land tenure.

To the Bantu and the Arabic-Berber states in the Sudan, there must be added two other such fields—the East Coast Sultanates and Abyssinia. In the first twenty years of the sixteenth century, the Portuguese, in establishing their early monopoly of the maritime trade between western Europe and the East Indies, the fruit of Vasco da Gama's enterprise, wrested the East Coast ports between the Limpopo and Cape Guardafui from the Arabs; and finding them more profitable than their earlier trading stations on the western coasts of the continent, made some efforts to colonize them and develop the interior. The Portuguese monopoly of the lucrative Indian trade was quickly challenged by Holland and England, and the knowledge of the east coast of Africa that came to Europe through the sea captains and merchants engaged in this trade is reflected in John Milton's *Paradise Lost*. For, when Adam (to console him for the loss of Paradise) is given a prophetic vision of 'all earth's kingdoms and their glory,' these sultanates were deemed by Milton sufficiently important to be included in it:

> Nor could his eye not ken
> The empire of Negus to his utmost post
> Ercoco, and the less maritime kings
> Mombasa, and Quiloa, and Melind,
> And Sofala, thought Ophir, to the realm
> Of Congo . . . .

With the colonisation of Africa by some European imperialist powers, its face and character have changed beyond recognition. Ivan Van

Sertima says: "No human disaster, with the exception of the Flood (if that biblical legend is true) can equal in dimension of destructiveness the cataclysm that shook Africa. We are all familiar with the slave trade and the traumatic effect of this on the transplanted black but few of us realize what horrors were wrought on Africa itself. Vast populations were uprooted and displaced, whole generations disappeared, European diseases descended like the plague, decimating both cattle and people, cities and towns were abandoned, family networks disintegrated, kingdoms crumbled, the threads of cultural and historical continuity were so savagely torn as under that henceforward one would have to think of two Africas: the one *before* and the one *after* the Holocaust."

Ngugi wa Thiong'o says: "Imperialism thus introduced mass poverty and cross regional underdevelopment . . . capitalism ensured poverty and mass starvation on a scale unknown before . . . capitalism by its [science and technology] uncontrolled use and exploitation of natural resources ensured the virtual dominance of nature over man by way of droughts and desertification . . . capitalism through its selective prescription of medical care, at least in the colonies, ensured a disease-ridden population who now lacked help from the herbalists and psychiatrists whose practices had been condemned as devilry. . . . Again Imperialism introduced literacy, but often confined it to clerks, soldiers, policemen, and the petty civil servants . . . the masses of African people could not read or write."[1] Africa became the continent of Calibans, the prince of Morocco and a Dark Continent.

Any study of African literature in India normally invites comparison with Indian literature. Critics suggest a theory that locks this study into the binary oppositions of colonizer/colonized, domination/resistance. But this experience of colonialism is not similar as the binary oppositions of postcolonial theory claim. Jan Mohamed talks of "the native whose economy and culture are destroyed."[2] It means that the colonizers designed the indigenous people of the Americas, Africa, and Australia and decided that they needed to be "civilized" and/or "exterminated." In this connection, Peter Worsley's comments are worth quoting:

> The colonial relationship was a relationship between societies, each of which had its own distinctive social institutions and its own internal social differences, its own culture and sub-cultures. Despite the political power of the conqueror, each colony was the product of a dialectic, a synthesis, not just a simple imposition, in which the social institutions and social values of the conquered

> was one of the terms of the dialectics. Histories of colonialism written by imperialists ignore one of these terms: history is the story of what the White man did. Nationalist historiography has developed a contrary myth: a legend of 'national' resistance which omits the uncomfortable fact of collaboration.[3]

India presents a different picture. Here, unlike Americas and Africa, the colonizer adopted the posture of non-interference with local customs, religious beliefs, cultural and legal systems, even in the face of demands for change by local interest groups. Therefore, literatures produced in India and Africa, though sharing some aspects of colonialism, are dissimilar in themes. Before embarking on a study of the African literature, especially the postcolonial literature, it is not irrelevant to examine Joseph Conrad and Graham Greene. They are Kipling and Forster of Africa. Conrad's *Heart of Darkness* was based on his voyage to the head-waters of the Congo and his personal impressions of the geographical and social conditions of that exploited country. Many of the characters were taken from life. Kurtz was suggested by one Klein, the company's agent at Stanley Falls. J.W. Beach says: "Kurtz is a personal embodiment, a dramatization, of all that Conrad felt of futility, degradation, and horror in what the Europeans in the Congo called 'progress,' which meant the exploitation of the natives by every variety of cruelty and treachery known to greedy man."[4] Marlow observes the 'natural' sounds of the sea and the physical vitality of the people who live by it:

> Now and then a boat from the shore gave one a momentary contact with reality. It was paddled by black fellows. You could see from afar the white of their eyeballs glistening. They shouted, sang; their bodies streamed with perspiration; they had faces like grotesque masks—these chaps; but they had bone, muscle, a wild vitality, an intense energy of movement, that was as natural and true as the surf along their coast. They wanted no excuse for being there. (61)

David Ward says: "This account has in it more than a vestige of the stereotypical prejudiced view of the European in Africa. The appeal to a natural, physical fitness in the alien race has a very long history in European thinking, stretching back to Montaigne's cannibals by way of Rousseau's noble savage. Conrad's own romantic temperament was just such as to be caught briefly by the glamour of the idea before probing beneath it."[5] Then, Conrad proceeds to unlock the European minds, full of profound fear of something unexplained at work in every mind. It was as if they were "travelling back to the earliest beginnings of the world, when vegetation rioted on the earth and the big trees were kings," (92-93) like visitors to a prehistoric world or an unknown planet. "We could have fancied ourselves the first of men taking possession of an accursed inheritance, to be subdued at the cost of profound anguish and of excessive toil." (95) David Ward says: "Ideas of mystery, ideas of darkness, ideas of godlike grandeur lurk here, such as those, hinted at in Kurtz's report to the International Society for the Suppression of Savage Customs projecting the imperial sway as an 'exotic Immensity ruled by an august Benevolence.' . . . Under the luminescence there is the real dark continent of 'Exterminate all the brutes,' (118) as Marlow finds in the margin of Kurtz's text. Yet further beneath that margin is that heart of the title, nothing to do with geographical centres, much more to do with a perceived failure of European civilization glimpsed through a continent of darkness in the mind." (11)

The difference between Conrad's and Greene's view of Africa is that the subtle questionings of the former are abandoned for an active enquiry into the operations of the imperial ideal. Conrad spared British imperialism reserving his wrath for European imperialisms—mainly the Belgian Congo—in relation to which he evokes a moral ideal for the British empire. Greene's work lacks the power of the Conradian imagery for colonial activity, but gains in compassion for the human experience of colonialism, a compassion for both parties to the encounter as individual lives trapped in a machine. In Greene's *Journey without Maps*, the emphasis is on dirt, disease, death, on woman as old, ugly, and naked, or as appealing "even to the European sexual taste and this is paradoxically by a genuine desire to unlearn, and to disregard imperial cartographers." The most powerful writing is contained in the following passage:

> Here you could measure what civilization was worth; . . . Civilization here remained exploitation. We had hardly, it seemed to me, improved the native lot at all, . . . They still drank from polluted water and suffered from the same worms. . . . Civilization was so far as Sierra Leon was concerned was the railway to Pendembu, the increased export of palm-nut; civilization, too, was Lever Brothers and the price they controlled; civilization was the long bar in the Grand, the sixpenny wages.[6]

Chinua Achebe of Nigeria says that Greene "is immeasurably superior to Joyce Cary, for instance, although the latter lived and worked in Africa for several years. Greene is not merely the greater artist; his insights are valued because he does not presume knowledge but writes tentatively as an outsider in his work set in Africa." Ngugi wa Thiong'o recalls his student days in Kenya in the 1950s when his fellow-students and friends in a class of English literature regarded Greene's work with reverence. He writes of Conrad: "Joseph Conrad always made me uneasy with his inability to see any possibility of redemption arising from the energy of the oppressed. Conrad wrote from the centre of the Empire."[7]

Jean-Paul Sartre, writing the Preface to Frantz Fanon's *The Wretched of the Earth*, says: "And when you have read Frantz Fanon's last chapter, you will be convinced that it would be better for you to be a native at the uttermost depths of his misery than to be a former settler." Africa is a vast continent and formulation of a general theory between say, Kenyan literature, Nigerian literature, South African literature and West African literature, would be premature but there are a few common denominators. To work these denominators out, even to list them, would be helpful, if not for the definition and theory of "African Literature." Janos Riesz, a German comparatist and defender of a new canon which would include "Third World Literature," has called Fanon's book a "classic." Fanon gave us important insights into the thematics of "Third World Literature": its treatment of colonialism and liberation, its rejection of Europe and implicitly the Western canon, its need for violence. One of his chapters is on literature, "O National Culture." In it Fanon delineated three stages for the development of "Third World Literature"/culture: (1) Pre-independence Literature: native intellectuals show that they have assimilated the culture of the occupying power; we might cite here negitude literature and the early pre-independence novel in Africa. (2) Literature "Of just-before-the-battle": the natives are restless. This literature is dominated by humour and allegory. Often, according to Fanon, this kind of literature is symptomatic of a period of distress and difficulty, where death is experienced, and disgust too. "We spew ourselves up; but underneath laughter can be heard." (3) Fighting literature, revolutionary literature: Fanon extensively cites the Guinean Keita Fodeba's "African Dawn" pointing out that "the understanding of the poem is not merely an intellectual advance, but a political advance."[8] Abdul JanMohamed names two phases of African literature, namely "dominant colonialism" which is overt, and, "hegemonic colonialism" which is covert.[9] It may be safely said that African Literature is resistance literature. Amulcar Cabral also says that it is a fighting literature, an opposition literature, a literature which deals with nation building, a literature which negates oppression.

After discussing two theoreticians of Africa—Fanon and Cabal—we pass on to Janos Riesz. He singles out five topics of interest which "Third World Literature" has in common: (1) The political and economic present: this would have to include the frequently scolded topicality found in plays such as *No More Oil Boom*, or *No Food No Country* by the Nigerian Junde Fatunde. (2) The colonial past: to which urgently needs to be added the neocolonial present, the theme of liberation and resistance. (3) Response to European or Western civilization: this is generally a rejection of the West including its canonized literary models but can also be a solidarity with Western progressive writers. (4) Literature issues: for example, orature versus literature, often bilingual, even polygot but in a meaningful way contrary to polygot aspects of the Euro-American modernist tradition. (5) Formation of the canon: subversion of the present canon and emphasis on canonical revision.

It would serve our purpose to elaborate our studies on five topics, mentioned above, one by one. To take our probe further on the first topic, we may go back to the 1950s, in South Africa. John C. Hawley says: "While colonial rule was gradually coming to an end throughout much of Africa during this decade, in South Africa, most whites were tightening their grip. Except in small 'native reserves' blacks could not own land and were thereby rendered economically dependent upon whites. Each main tribal group was provided with a 'homeland' (a 'Bantustan'), and they were encouraged by the white government to declare their independence. Consequently, within South Africa, where they worked, they could thereby be considered 'foreign natives' and/or 'immigrants' who had no political rights outside the homeland. . . . Black writers sought to reverse this trend by alerting whites to their frustration, and by raising the consciousness of other blacks."[10]

Ayi Kwei Armah, in his book *The Beautyful Ones Are Not Yet Born*, charges Nkrumah with clinging to power beyond his youthfulness; overstaying his welcome and usefulness; frustrating younger Ghanaians who wanted to take over; running a corrupt government, letting the colonial heritage fall to pieces.

The extremely repressive conditions in postcolonial Uganda under first Idi Amin, then Milton Obote, and the resulting mass exodus of both Asians and intellectuals from the country, would seem to be fertile ground for Ugandan writers on par with that of Kenya. Indeed, one poem by Ugandan author and cultural critic Taban lo Liyong counsels the nation's youth to fight with a pen instead of a sword. George Heron sees Okot p'Bitek's "Song of a Soldier" as representative of frustration of Ugandan writers: "It is a very terrible book because I lost quite a lot of relatives in the Uganda coup, a lot of friends, too, and after I write a few lines, I drop it because it causes a lot of tears."[11]

Ngugi wa Thiong'o is East Africa's most celebrated author and a Kenyan. He exposes the hypocrisy, corruption and brutality of postcolonial Kenya in English language novels, *A Grain of Wheat*, and *Petals of Blood*, and also in Gikuyu-language play, *Nagaahika Ndeenada* (I Will Marry When I Want). He criticised the President of independent republic of Togo in West Africa, who celebrated 1984 with the President of West German Federal Council, Franz Joseph Strauss: "And so 1884, which is always remembered by millions of African people as the year of historic shame, the start of a century of continuous humiliation of Africa by the West, is being celebrated with pride by an African President."[12] There are other absurdities. "Mobuto of Zaire, in an act of supreme African authenticity, has ceded a whole territory many times the size of New Zealand to a West German rocket company. A group of African leaders recently begged France to send troops to Chad to protect French legitimate interests, threatened by 'imperialist Libya.' Moi of Kenya has given military bases to U.S.A. without a debate in parliament, with Kenyans only later learning about the 'secret' deal through a debate in US Congress."[13]

Coming to the second topic, viz., the literature of liberation and resistance, we, once again, look at South African literature, first of all. A journal, *Drum*, founded in 1951, provided a home for an impressive array of black writers, and Nat Nakasa's *Classic*, founded in 1963, printed a great deal of their best work. In 1978, a new journal *Staffrider* caught the contemporary spirit. Among black writers, Bessie Head, Andre Brink, Oswald Mtshali, Mongane Serote, Njabulo Ndebele, Mandelenkosi, Langa, Mafika Gwala, Don Mattera, D.M. Zwelonke, and a host of writers write against racial oppression, and apartheid. Many black writers, like Dan Jacobsen, Sydney Clouts, Christopher Hope and Roy Macnab, had chosen to leave South Africa and went into exile. Dennis Brutus (b. 1924) in *Sirens, Knuckles, Boots* (1963) and *Thoughts Abroad* (1970), has been one of those who argue that the most honest South African literature must be that of the exile, written, as it is, away from the compromises that have been necessary for publication within the country. Among some exiled groups, autobiography is often the chosen genre. Peter Abrahams's *Tell Freedom* (1954), and Mphahlele's *Down Second Avenue* (1959) are two examples of this genre. Among short story writers, La Guma and Richard Rive are the most popular figures.

In Kenya, the most popular writer is Ngugi wa Thiong'o. He is a writer of resistance. On the other hand, Gakaara wa Wanjau was detailed for four years for his pro-Mau Mau and nationalist writing in Kiswahili and Gikuyu. Then, he was detained in 1986 in postcolonial Kenya "for alleged association with 'Mwakenya' underground movement, but was released after signing an officially prepared false 'confession' in which he repudiated his works, including his prize winning diary."[14] His writing became increasingly critical of the postcolonial Kenyan government and elite.

Within West African fiction, Amos Tutuola's *The Palm-Wine Drinkard* (1953) is the first work to posit and explore the feeling of estrangement engendered by the colonial encounter. His writing in English enabled West African writers not only to explore the disabling features of colonialism but also to evoke a postcolonial future within the colonial present.

When we examine the third topic, we quote George M. Gugelberger, an important third world theoretician. He says: "The negative response to Europe (for example, Fanon or more recent and very vocal Plan-Africanist defenders, such as Chinweizu, is a transitory stage which emphasizes race . . . since the advent of neocolonialism, however, it has become increasingly clear that the true and progressive third world writer wants to connect with progressive writers elsewhere. . . . A glance at the reception of Brecht in Cuba, Colombia, Brazil, the Philippines, Nigeria, Guinee (for example, Alioum Fantoure's use of a Brecht ballad in the heart of his novel *Tropical Circle*) but above all Kenya (especially the case of Ngugi wa Thiong'o) demonstrates this."[15] The Brazilian Augusto Boal, in his *Theatre of the Oppressed*, says: "The poetics of the oppressed is essentially the poetics of liberation: The spectator frees himself, thinks and acts for himself. Theatre is action. Perhaps the theatre is not revolutionary itself; but have no doubts, it is a rehearsal of revolution."[16] Boal further says: "it [essence] is designed to bridle the individual, to adjust him to what preexists; . . . if on the contrary, we want to stimulate the spectator to transform his society, to engage in revolutionary action, in that case we will have to seek another poetics." (47) The third world writers have sought Brecht's poetics for their purpose, wherein social being determines thought, man is alterable, history central, and reason more important than emotion.

As far as the matter of the Western canons is concerned, the African writers adopted and rejected them, as we find in India. Chinua Achebe's novel *Things Fall Apart*, like that of R.K. Narayan's novels, has adopted the linear plot development, whereas Wole Soyinka, in his novel *The Interpreters*, has, like Salman Rushdie, dispensed with plot. Ngugi, in his novels *The River Between* and *Weep Not, Child*, uses a linear plot, whereas in his later novel *A Grain of Wheat*, he deviates from this Western canon of a plot. One Tanzanian playwright and novelist, Penina Muhando Mlama, says that theatre in Africa must arise from indigenous "oral literary and performative forms" rather than imported Western dramatic traditions.

This leads to the fourth point, viz., the language issue. Since the writing of *Decolonising the Mind* by Ngugi, the language issue has dominated the critical discourse on African literature, with intellectuals like Abiola Irele defending and expanding Ngugi's position and others, like Chinua Achebe, Wole Soyinka and Lewis Nkosi, challenging the efficacy, relevance, and political expediency of writing literature in African language. Still, the basic tenets of Ngugi's argument, as outlined in *Decolonising the Mind* and *Moving the Centre*, remain compelling: that, by writing in English, French, or Portuguese, African authors enrich their languages and cultures at the cost of impoverishing or even, endangering their own; that European languages are not only inadequate for expressing African concerns and experiences, but also carry with them the ideological baggage of slavery and colonialism; and that Europhone African literature automatically excludes the majority of African people from its audience. But the Sudanese writer, domiciled in Uganda, questions Ngugi's faith in translation as the key to a viable Afrophone literature and says that important components of African languages (i.e., praise names) cannot be translated into Western languages.

Language has been a hot issue in East African literature ever since coastal poets made the switch from Arabic to Kiswahili in their literary compositions. In the late eighteenth century, Abu Bakari concluded his epic poem "Utenzi wa Katirifu" by stating that "his purpose had been to tell an Arabic tradition in the vernacular (Ki'ajami)."[17] At that time, Arabic, as the language of a foreign imperialist power and world religion, was to Kiswahili as English, French, Portuguese are to it and other African languages today. That the switch from the Arabic to Kiswahili was soon followed by "The Golden Age of Classical Swahili Literature"[18] augurs well for the proposed move from a Europhone to an Afrophone African literature.

We come to the last topic. In what sense is Achebe's *Things Fall Apart* a response to and/or correction of Conrad? Doubts about Western representations of other cultures increasingly lead to the study of "testimonial literature." As to the difference between Achebe and Conrad, Achebe says:

> I went to a good school modelled on British public schools. I read lots of English books. . . . The savages arrayed against him [white man] were sinister and stupid, or, at most, cunning. I hated their guts. . . . But . . . (later) I realized . . . I was not on Marlow's boat steaming up the Congo in *Heart of Darkness*. I was one of those strange beings jumping up and down on the river bank, making horrid faces. Or, if I insisted on the boat-ride, then I had to settle perhaps for that "improved specimen," as Conrad sarcastically calls him, more absurd than a dog in a pair of breeches trying to make out the witchcraft behind the ship's water-gauge.[19]

The main thrust of the writing project in postcolonial Africa has been the authentication of "those strange beings jumping up and down" but on their own terms: from the Africans's view of their world. In order to be truly representative of the people, Malama and other African intellectuals like Ngugi and Amandina Lihamba, a Tanzanian playwright, have collaborated with everyday African people, many of them are illiterate and live in rural areas, to produce a literature that is popular in its origins as well as its destination. In theatre, for instance, Mlama insists, it must arise from indigenous "oral literary and performative forms." This incorporation of oral forms into common peoples's theme, including women, constituted a kind of testimonial literature. Although this kind of testimonial literature mainly based itself on the form of an autobiographical narrative, it also included in its fold popular theatre. This literature is, therefore, often collaborative, multivocal, and documentary. This literature was a collaboration between a radicalized (Marxist) intelligentsia with the subaltern. Written from the perspective of the marginalized and oppressed, testimonial literature is intended to serve as a corrective to official, hegemonic versions of history. For instance, an extraordinary volume of Mau Mau-themed novels, plays, poetry, and memoirs have been published since independence of Kenya. Writers like J.M. Kariuki, Gakaara wa Wanju, Karari Njama, Guen Gikoyo, Joram

Wamweya and Koboi Muriithi (to name but a few) sought to break the national silence on the subject of Mau Mau and to erect a literary memorial to their struggles.

To conclude our studies of African literature, we can start re-examining Conrad's *Heart of Darkness* and Cary's *Mister Johnson*. The study of the European novel of Africa should continue, but only alongside the study of the African novel of Africa as well as the African novel of Europe and the United States. In India, we study not only Narayan, Anand, Rao, Rushdie, but also Kipling, Forster, Scott, and Mason. Christopher Miller's *Blank Darkness: Africanist Discourse in French*, Dorothy Hammond and Alta Jablow's *The Africa That Never Was: Four Centuries of British Writing about Africa*, and JanMohammed's *Manichean Aesthetics: The Politics of Literature in Colonial Africa*, among others, are beginnings in that direction. We must not forget to read Chinweizu's *The West and the Rest of US*, a ground-breaking work, like Edward Said's *Orientalism*.

NOTES

1. Ngugi wa Thiong'o, *Decolonising the Mind* (London: James Carry, 1986), pp. 66-67.
2. Abul R. JanMohamed "The Economy of Manichean Allegory: The Function of Racial Difference in Colonialist Literature," in *"Race," Writing and Difference*, ed. Henry Louis Gates, Jr. (Chicago: Univ. of Chicago Press, 1986), p. 79.
3. Peter Worsley, *The Three Worlds: Culture and World Development* (Chicago: Univ. of Chicago Press, 1984), p. 4.
4. J.W. Beach, *The Twentieth Century Novel* (Ludhiana: Lyall, 1965), p. 343.
5. David Ward, *Chronicles of Darkness* (London: Routledge, 1989), p. 8.
6. Graham Greene, *Journey without Maps* (London: Heinemann, 1936), pp. 60-61.
7. Ngugi wa Thiong'o "Moving the Centre: Towards a Pluralism of Cultures," *The Journal of Commonwealth Literature*, Vol. XXVI, No. 1, 1991, p. 202.
8. Frantz Fanon, *The Wretched of the Earth* (Penguin, 1967), pp. 179 and 186.
9. Abdul R. JanMohamad, "The Economy of Manichean Allegory," p. 80.
10. John C. Hawley, "South African Writing in English," *English Postcoloniality: Literatures from around the World*, ed. Radhika Mohanram and Gita Rajan (Westport: Greenwood Press, 1996), p. 56.

11. Okot p'Bitek, quoted in George Heron's "Uganda" in *In European Language Writing in Sub-Saharan Africa*, Vol. 2, ed. Albert S. Gerald (Budapest: Akademia Kiado/UNESCO, 1986), p. 947.
12. Ngugi wa Thiong'o, *Decolonising the Mind*, p. 79.
13. *Ibid*, pp. 79-80.
14. Ann Bierstecker, "An Alternative East African Voice: The Wa-Nduta Stories of Gakaara Wa Wanjau," *Research in African Literature*, 22.4 (1991), p. 75.
15. "Decolonizing the Canon," p. 518.
16. Augusto Boal, *Theatre of the Oppressed* (New York, 1985), p. 155.
17. Albert S. Gerald, *African-Language Literatures: An Introduction to the Literary History of Sub-Saharan Africa* (Washington D.C.: Three Continents Press, 1981), p. 98.
18. *Ibid.*
19. Chinua Achebe, "African Literature as Restoration of Celebration," quoted in Anthonia Kalu's "Between Cultures: Insights on West African Writing in English," in *English Postcoloniality*, p. 85.

The Lace and Jewels of Eastern African Traditionalism

TABAN IO LIYONG

Decolonisation, as I take it, was meant to be total. That is: political decolonisation first; economic decolonisation next and finally cultural decolonisation. Putting it in that order is deceptive for we have not lost our culture at all. Our culture had been removed from the public arena to the private. And therefore political decolonisation was also to free our culture from the backroom to the frontroom, from being covert to overt. And, this cultural decolonisation was to be carried out by us, according to what we are and were. And what we would like to be: the image of ourselves that strides before us like a shadow.

For me, the farthest back we could go to ground our cultural base are the golden ages of each African peoples. That is as far back as the time we were on the ascent at the time when, or just before, the coloniser came and stilled our drums, stopped our dance. That time was no dark age. In West Africa, the high watermarks of Ghana, Mali, Songhai are there before us. As are the Yoruba Nok culture, and Ife origin. In the Sudan we had the Fur, Fung, Shilluk high civilizations. In Uganda the Bachwezi streaked across the land like a comet. Bunyoro, Buganda, Ankole, Rwanda, Urundi were left in its wake. In Tanzania, the Engaruka terraced farming testifies to a high agricultural industry where a people stayed put and harnessed seasonal water to serve a sedentary community. In Zimbabwe Monomotapa built the monuments that testify to high civilization and mastery of physics. In the republican lands, that is people without kings and queens, the environment-conscious Nuer, Dinka, Maasai and Gikuyu (they became agriculturalists later) man, beasts; land and water were used to the credit of man. In all these cultures there are things we call ours; there are ways we call ours; there are beliefs we call ours; there are aspirations we call ours which our ancestors created, which standards were so high that the passage of time has not corroded them. Whatever we remember from the past is a remnant of a high monument that has been worn down by time.

To call for the return to the high watermarks, to envisage the return and reinstitution of the high level of our past is but the normal thing all cultural nationalists demand for their people. We could call it a demand for our rebirth, the rebirth of the ways, our ways, the cultures of our people.

The word renaissance has been misused twice before: one in Harlem of the twenties and another in nineteenth century England. The Harlem renaissance of the twenties by the Blacks of Harlem—which glorious past were they recalling? Meroitic? Theban? Alexandrian? Songhaian? Malian? or Ghanaian? The other time was when Walter Pater and other Victorians rechristened the Humanistic spirit of the middle ages as a period of Renaissance. This period, as you will recall, came after Europe got wisened up fighting the Crusades. And, the ancient Greek (and Egyptian and African) books that had been translated and kept by the Arabs found their way into Europe. The European princes had come through Italy and Greece to fight the wars in the Levant.

Now, which period in that vast past could Europe claim as its roots? Pagan Roman? Pagan Greek? Pagan Egypt? Pagan Mesopotamia? For, Christianity was still young. If anything, humanism was anti-Christianity and pro-pagan. Unless Walter Pater had detected that the princes of the Church were pitted against the Pagan heritage of the East, and vied with it, and sought to create their own monuments inspired by Christianity to dwarf the achievements of the Arabs, Romans, Greeks, and Egyptians?

When the colonisers, both Muslim Arabs and Christian Europeans, disengaged from the Crusades, they turned their attention to Africa. From Morocco the Almoravids came and destroyed Ghana, Mali, Songhai. Then the Portuguese came from the sea, followed by the French and British and Spaniards. And they made Africans and Almoravids captives. Had the whiteman come to assist us along the lines we were then treading, who knows where we would have been by now? Or where the whiteman would have been? But, time was frozen, all our seeds were infected, and retarded children were grudgingly born.

The classical culture of Egypt, the first civilization in the world created by the efforts of our people; the classical culture of Meroe, the second highest civilization of Africans, the Coptic culture of Egypt, Sudan, Ethiopia which spilled over into Kenya, Uganda, Tanzania, all of these need to be reborn, need their renaissance. As do the cultures of the Igbo,

Yoruba, Akan, Bambara.

Renaissance is a sweet word. But does it happen by itself? A felt hunger, thirst, need or it has to be felt. The feeling of orphanage, of deprivation, has to be there. The need to do something about it has to follow. The plighting of troth to it; the utter dedication to its return, dedication to bringing it about, have to be there.

I take it that when Kwame Nkrumah paraphrased Jesus by saying seek ye first the political kingdom and all shalt be added unto ye, he had in mind that the political leaders would do all the adding. And haven't they added to the sum-total of our burden? But I think it is time we added things unto ourselves; we should look at the rubbish heap of history, at the backyard of our homes and minds for things to be rescued, cleaned and rehabitated.

Through Oral Traditions of all sorts: in history, in religion, in philosophy, in politics and administration, in literature, we had had glimpses of classical Africa which we have appreciated enough to urge us to woo her and bring her back into our new homesteads. Leading back from the tendrils of African migration where we now are through the various adventitious branches upto the boles and roots down the Nile or up the Niger, we are all legitimate heirs to Africa's past racially, linguistically, religiously, culturally. In fact our individual claims to any African classical period is more justified than that of, say, a Northern European like the Dutch Erasmus to the classical cultures of the Levant. For apart from Catholic Christianity, aren't Athens and Amsterdam worlds apart? And, in a later age, did Christianity make the Dutch in South Africa see a common humanity with the Africans?

We have greater claims even to classical Greek culture which was an expansion of our Egyptian roots. Which was an elaboration, and much more to the point, a publicity of the knowledge of the philosopher of Egypt by the publicity-conscious Greeks, by Greeks who broadcasted aloud the secret knowledge of the savants of Egypt. Greek civilization was a "renaissance" of the African civilization of Egypt. All pre-Aristotelian major Greek philosophers save Socrates had been to Egypt, had done post-graduate studies in Egypt. This list includes the great Pythagoras, the great Archimedes, and the greatest of them all, Plato. After Socrates died, Plato came to Egypt and studied there for ten years. It was only when he was ready to write his Socratic dialogues and found his university that he returned to Athens. So, we should have no qualms at all in crossing the Aegean Sea to claim an Attic renaissance. If we do not do it, it is because we have not seen it clearly. Otherwise, science, civilization, do not hold any mysteries to us: we saw them when they were young: we had given them birth. And, what had grown in our soil once can be raised afresh, can be replanted, can take roots again. We should therefore aim at building African pyramids, mark II.

Subjects taught at school are supposed to enlighten us, especially the cultural subjects such as history, literature, religion, culture. They are supposed to help one to attain a high level of general awareness, of understanding, of *kurundo* as we say in Kuku language. That is when one has reached the age of discriminating between good and bad, right and wrong, what is and what is not.

But society also hopes there would arise excellent students who would not only master the old songs, but would also know the techniques of prosody and compose new songs, replenish the old stock. The Acholi, when judging a traditional case, used 'palaver' a lot, citing previous cases and instances, called *ongon*. That way they argued out matters of ethics and aesthetics.

Is it asking too much if we say that there should be practical aspects to the Oral Tradition courses? That we should have new griots to arise who would put our old and current history into a recitative song? That we should have able raconteurs to record their final examination stories on television? That a workshop be organised to criticize oral performances of students by their 'uneducated' elders? That it is not enough to offer a course in Oral Literature if the students do not go out as performers using the old forms as well?

So, the cultural subjects are functional, as are the social sciences. And, the acquisition of expertise or knowledgeability that we had traditionally acquired very formally was meant to inculcate into us the old ways, songs, and knowledge, as well as speed us along to new creations.

So, Oral literature is a functional subject. Through it we learn all about African culture and outlook to the world. We hear songs, learn them; we hear folktales, learn them, retell them; we hear epics, see some heroic songs composed (or adapted) and learn to compose our own. We also hear philosophy, as high as they had radiated out from Upper Egypt. We learn house-building (otherwise given the megalomaniac title of 'architecture') and practice it. We hear cases and participate in questioning and cross-examining, as well as passing sentence. As far as politics is concerned, no social science was more developed. The choice of the bride to become queen, the upbringing of princes and princesses, the method of rule, the termination of a rule and ascension of another ruler, all these were meticulously laid out and followed. In the acephalus communities where age-grades were assigned various grades of responsibilities one finds that the succession issues that face modern African republics have all been resolved.

It is sheer intellectual unresourcefulness that has kept the noses of our political scholars glued to their Greek, Roman, British, French, American, German, Russian textbooks. They trust the written word so much; they know how to read, write and footnote so much, they have forgotten how to hear, retain, cogitate, and discuss. They never rebelled enough.

When I reached the age of understanding, of *kurundo*, I threw away my Christian name, as Okot had done his before me, and as Ngugi was to do after us. But Okot, despite all the wisdom of Lawino, never took practical steps to become an African believer in a traditional African religion. In his Oxford University days he had flirted with socialism and logical positivism and this seems to have kept him away from any religion since then: he remained a sceptic. Ngugi, when he went to Northwestern University, became a Black Power respector. I think his socialism was reawakened in him, the socialism that he had absorbed in Leeds from Professor Arnold Kettle. Besides, his childhood sympathy for the poor, the deprived, came back to him when he was old enough to see those same treatments being meted out to Africans by fellow Africans. In short, he remained a socialist. And the nearest he could come to being Africanised is in the adoption of Gikuyu for telling his socialist morality stories. As for me, when I first went to school in 1945, I had a copper/bronze bangle on my wrist. My first teacher, Ogwang Chakngwec told me to leave it at home. Now I carry with me an icon—down in my purse!

I do not see why Gikuyu language should be studied if it cannot later be put to the creation of modern *marabeta* songs. I cannot see why Gikuyu language should be studied and not used for crating new and modern folktales: folktales with modern messages. I do not see why Gikuyu language should be learnt and not used for extending the English form of the novel.

The only reason why initiation stories and songs should be studied at school is to help us see the mystical significance, the moral restraint, the courage-building poems within the initiation rites that our people had created. And this can be done whilst preparing the students for initiation or explaining to them the mystery they had just undergone. I am all for a return to our rites of passage from the ringing of bell, striking of light, pinching of the bottom, and tasting of alcohol at birth, to the three-four days lying in, then puberty, marriage, old age, death. With all the attendant religious and social duties.

I cannot see a reason why an African, disenchanted with Christianity, should build for himself a break-away church instead of returning to worship God Ngai under the *mugumo* tree. We lived this long without the benefit or handicap of Christianity. Christianity is but an icing on the colonial cake. When a Kikuyu girl exclaims "Ngai!" I hope it is our ancestral God she is invoking rather than the substitute God, Jehovah.

In the law-books I hope the anathema placed round the words 'witch,' 'witch-craft,' 'wizard,' 'magic' are removed and our healers and seers—*olaibon* in Maasai, *'bunit'* in Kuku *abunat* (pl.) in Coptic—are regarded with all the dignity accorded to other priests. Sometimes, the unbelievers in our religions want us to explain the mysteries of our faiths to their satisfaction. To their satisfaction? When they themselves have not explained the mysteries in their faiths to their own satisfaction? When they have settled to muddle along with mysteries of (a) divine conception, (b) four-Gods-in-one (the fourth is Virgin Mary), (c) Eucharistic feast, (d) Judas as a cursed or divine tool? The Shilluk divine kings do not die. They ascend to heaven in a smoke form. How different is that from the mystery surrounding the death and ascension of Jesus Christ? The Yoruba new king eats a portion of the old and dead king to ensure legitimate succession. If that is cannibalism what do the Christians do every Sunday?

Oral literature is but one of the vistas from the Ivory Tower through which we can cast a glance down to the beautiful world Ngai had laid out before Gekoyo na Mumbi. It remains for us to repossess it, re-occupy it, re-own it. It remains for us to dive into it, drown in it, die in it to be born anew, reborn with more commitment to purify the house of all foreign accretions, and populate it with all the artifacts that had belonged to it, all the awe and aura that had belonged to our Godhead. It remains for us to revisit *The River Between* again, and see if Makuyu should not recover the other ridge across the Chania River as well. It remains for us to see why Mumbi should have desired Christening at all. Why not learn technology without disturbing one's religious, cultural base?

Okot tells of when, after he had left Oxford, Makerere University wanted to establish an Institute of African Studies for him to head. He scoffed at the idea. According to him, the whole university in an African nation should be the institution for the study of the Africans and their ways. I agree with him.

Oral literature could broadly cover all the areas of thought, knowledge, skills orally transmitted by our people and aurally received by them. This would cover such areas as ideas, beliefs, legends, histories, traditions in science, medicine, building, farming, astronomy, etc. Of course, at a very literal level, we would cover folktales: legends, poems/songs, proverbs, tongue-twisters, epics, hymns.

It is when you are standing with your two feet firmly on African culture that you can create artefacts that are extensions of the ethics and aesthetics of African way of life.

It may be ambitious, it may be impertinent, but, all the same, the question must be asked: Is the Literature Departments ready for the next revolution? Is KOLA (Kenya Oral Literature Association) ready to take over all the Literature Departments? All the History Departments? All the Geography Departments? All the Architecture Departments? All the Institutes of African Studies? Is KOLA ready to do all these as a prelude to converting the National Universities into Advanced Institutions for the Study of the African, his past and present conditions, and an active dedication to the recovery of our first place in civilization? Can we vow to reconnect with Zinjanthropus? With Egypt? With Meroe?

If we can't do that then we do not know history and should not mouth the word decolonisation.

"Nowhere and Everywhere": Reconstruction of Nation in African-Canadian Writers

NEERJA JAYAL CHAND

What is a Nation? In an essay entitled "What is a Nation," Ernest Renan gives his oft-quoted concept of Nation in these words: "A Nation is a soul, a spiritual principle. Two things, which in truth are but one, constitute this soul or spiritual principle. One lies in the past, one in the present. One is the possession in common of a rich legacy of memories; the other is present-day consent, the desire to live together, the will to perpetuate the value of the heritage that one has received in an undivided form. . . . To have common glories in the past and to have a common wish to perform still more—these are the essential conditions for being a people."[1]

Canadian writers in English have faced a perpetual dilemma, typical of most colonial literary situations: Without a definable Nation and National identity and character, no national literature would develop, but without a National literature, a National identity and character may never emerge at all! The writer's task is therefore twofold, to build as well as to image a nascent Nation which has a strong native tradition of its own in the past, along with an ever inflowing stream of immigrants, from all parts of the world, with their divergent cultural baggages, in the present. A large body of recent Canadian literature has, consciously or unconsciously, taken up the challenge and addressed this dilemma directly or indirectly. African-Canadian literature is a significant portion of this large body of Canadian literature.

African-Canadian literature in English is a vibrant output of writings by "Canadian writers of African descent,"[2] mostly immigrants from an endless list of countries like Trinidad, Jamaica, Barbados, Ghana, Haiti, Kenya, Nigeria, South Africa, Guyana, Zimbabwe, United States of America, and from within Canada itself. These writers write out "a collective African consciousness," despite the diversity of their cultural backgrounds, a consciousness embodied in the fabric of oral traditions, woven from one generation to the next, through myths, storytelling, fables, proverbs, rituals, worksongs and sermons meshed with Western literary forms, observes Aynna Black.

African-Canadian literary form has existed for at least two centuries, and began with the importation of slaves in Quebec and the arrival of American Slaves in Nova Scotia and Southern Ontario. According to George Elliott Clarke's *Fire on the Water: An Anthology of Black Nova Scotian Writings*, the texts of Nova Scotian John Marrant, a former slave, date back to 1785, and are the earliest known writings of a black living in Canada. The more recent influx of immigrants from the Caribbean to Canada in the nineteen-fifties, sixties and seventies and largely the arrival of Africans, has created an even more highly textured literary quilt or mosaic. Coming from diverse roots and cultural contexts, the writers have reacted divergently to their situation as "writers of colour" in Canada. Surprisingly enough, even though these writers have been in Canada for over two hundred years, they are still regarded as newcomers. No wonder, a sense of "not belonging" is common to almost all of them. In the words of Claire Harris, a black Canadian poet from Trinidad, the marginalization of the blacks in Canada is the outcome of "a blatant ethnocentricity [which] condemns people of color to the sidelines: eternal immigrants for ever poised on the verge of *not belonging.*"[3]

Cyril Dabydeen, a Canadian poet from Guyana has a poem in the Strathocna that he calls "Lady Icarus." The poem is about Maria from Ecuador who comes seeking a new life in Canada and is held in the Strathcona. Maria tries to escape deportation but

> Your rope
> of sheets and blankets
> broke
> no sun now melting wax
> your hold snaps
> as you plunge
> to sudden death
> we stand on guard for thee
> Oh so glorious and free
> O Canada, O Canada.[4]

Maria is getting her reward, as if, for aspiring to live under the Canadian sky. The Icarus allusion symbolizes overreaching, the satiric intent of the last two lines is implicit in their echo of the national anthem. This is how Canada 'welcomes' a coloured immigrant.

Once in Canada, the African-Canadians are relegated to the margins by virtue of their colour and soon begin to see colour as an issue. Carmen Rodriguez, Latin American by birth, expresses this realization in these words: "Since living in Canada I have been forced to see something that I had never seen before: colour. In Chile I did not have a colour. I was like everybody else. Colour was not an issue. Here I have been forced to see myself as a dark woman, a woman of colour."[5]

Intensely aware of the Otherness of an Afrosporic immigrant in Canada, Arnold Harrichand Itwaru, poet, novelist, critic, who was born in Guyana and has been living in Toronto since 1969, conveys forcefully his anger, frustration and anguish as an immigrant belonging to an ethnic minority in Canada and lashes out against the supposed bigotry, hegemony and exploitation prevalent in Canada, thereby deconstructing its official image or self-image as a land of equal opportunity, justice and humanitarianism. The entire focus of his book *The Invention of Canada*[6] is on the Thematization of Racism in the works of Post World War II immigrant writers in Canada where he underscores the glaring contrast between Canada's national slogans like unity in diversity and multiculturalism and questions Canada's official claim that minorities in the country can fully participate in national life and at the same time retain their distinctive traditions. Itwaru argues that this claim conflicts directly with the cultural institutions of the mainstream white dominant anglophone Canada. Deeply disturbed by what he calls the "demonization and dehumanization" of the African in Canada, Itwaru cries out in rage and despair:

> The enslavement of the African, the mortified hated other, segregated and subjugated, the agonized body configured in subservient labour, negrified subhuman, though less in the magnitude of numbers and the duration of years of horror than in the regions of the Caribbean and southern U.S.A. was still enacted in Canada where the demonization and the dehumanization of the African person was part of the callous legacy in which the Racism of "white supremacy," the edifice of the Great White North is firmly entrenched. The *denigration of the African in Canada*, prevalent today, is the expression of another drawn out anguish, another cruel Othering.[7]

Other voices of Afrosporic Canadian writers are however not so anguished and vehemently pessimistic. If there are minor and major writers of Afriean origin exposing or trying to expose the myth of multiculturalism and also resisting the subtle or overt pressure of assimilation with the dominant culture and its Anglophone discourse, there is an equal number of writers of colour who choose to project multirooted, multitechnic even multiphrenic pan Canadian image and refuse to be pigeonholed into the strait and suffocating category of "minority immigrant writers." These writers realise fully well that ethnic purism is both impractical and obstructionist in the process of nation-building and does not help anyone at all. Also, culture is not a static phenomenon. It changes because change is part of growth, of being living cells instead of fossils or dead wood.

Such writers, immigrant, Afrosporic, Otimistic, have existed in Canada all along. Being coloured, they do write about themselves, but Racism is not the main issue. It is a small fraction of their work. A brief look at some such writers, including one or two who have just hit the scene, is very assuring.

Reshard Wy-El Gool (1931-1989), part Persian, part-Malay, born in a family that had roots in India and South Africa, was educated in England and came to Canada in 1964 to study and teach political philosophy, lived "in the centre of an interesting—if chaotic—world of ideas, literature, politics, the arts and the community—whichever community he happened to be in at the moment."[8] His poems in this volume are reflections, revelations as well as extensions of a rich, varied and complicated life and are located in Persia, Paris, Kentucky, Crete, Germany, South Africa, Canada—his allusions ranging from Greek myth, Donne, John Stuart Mill to Braque Charlie Parker, Martin Luther King and like all good poetry, move from the very personal to more abstract themes of love, life and death. His second novel *The Nemesis Casket* in the words of Uma Parameswaran asserts a pan-Canadian consciousness and confidence.[9] Each of the narrators in the novel, like Gool himself, is a product of at least three races and cultures, representing a pan-Canadian identity and sensibility which is a fact of life for such a large number of Canadians that it is not only futile but ludicrous to insist on pigeonholing them or their roots to any one particular source. Deborah Allen, in her introduction to the album containing excerpts from *The Nemesis Casket* read by the author says: "The *Nemesis Casket* is an elaborate undertaking, a mosaic of voices that links Canada to its parts and to the third world." Using polyphonic voices, interracial relationships and regional landscapes the novel which is repository of History, narrativizes Canada's multiculturalism. In a critique of Canadian Broadcasting Corporation Gool had pointed out that literature, like a national broadcasting network, should "show and celebrate" cultural differences while preserving the Nemesis Casket. His own novel does just that.

In her introduction to the much acclaimed anthology *The Geography of Voice*, Diana McGifford says: "The alienation of the immigrant and the bitter stings of racism"[10] are the two painful realities shaping the lives and art of South Asian Canadian. This indictment is generally considered to be applicable to the African-Canadian writers also. M.G. Vassanji who belongs to both these categories, being a hybrid product of Cutch-Gujarat, Kenya-East Africa and Toronto-Canada however chooses (unlike Itwaru) to not to address the issue of Racism directly. In his three novels *The Gunny Sack* (1989), *No New Land* (1991), *The Book of Secrets* (1995) and one book of short stories *Uhuru Street* (1992) Vassanji creates a fictional community of immigrants called Shamsis who like the writer himself in Canada, come from East Africa and have ancestral roots and memory in India. The creation of a community is almost a literary strategy because in its multicultural diversity, multiracial ethnic disparity and multipheric pluralism, this community represents a Nation within a nation, a microcosmic pan Canadian identity at a macro level and demolishes any narrow, sectarian notions of colour and Racism. In an unpublished paper entitled "Creative Conflicts: Multiculturalism in the Mind," Vassanji makes his literary agenda—if one may call it so—very clear: "In my novels, I have traced the evolution of community man—from a person circumscribed by the relationships, faith and mores of a small community, with an implicit acceptance of life's contradictions and ironies and ambiguous identities to such a person in the western metropolis with a conscious acknowledgement and acceptance—even celebration—of these ambiguities."[11] Vassanji's novelistic preoccupations are similar to Reshard Gool's whom he admires as a writer and who also uses the same word "celebration" with reference to cultural differences ("show and celebrate").

Apart from these few, a very large number of other major and minor Anglophone African-Canadian writers[12] are writing an Afrocentric, self-reflexive diasporic discourse, writing, in the words of Claire Harris, "to rehabilitate the Black person, her beauty, her smile, her walk, her genius . . . his too," and "to explore the reality of a Canadian society," and in it find a Canadian sky of their own. One must mention two very recent young African-Canadian voices, Iqbal Ian Rashid who was born in Dar Es-Salam, Tanzania in 1965, raised in Toronto and published his third book of poetry, *The Heat Yesterday* in 1995. His earlier book *Black Markets White Boyfriends* (1992) was nominated for Canada's Gerald Lampert Prize. As an African-Canadian gay poet, he represents a minority within a minority and his sexual preferences deepen and sharpen his painful experiences as a writer of colour in Canada. In a poem entitled *A Redefinition*, he writes

> You reach for me, large
> white spider against my darkness and I am
> yours, now and for the first time.
> for you see, my big, blonde, perfume-soaked Sahib,
> you have, through your polite—your civilised—grace,
> brought down my New world.[13]

On the other end of the spectrum we have a volatile young immigrant writer from Zimbabwe who shot into fame with her first novel Nehanda[14] (1994). Yvonne Vera was born in Bulawayo, Zimbabwe and now lives in Canada. She situates her novel in a remote village in Zimbabwe where a newly born girl Nehanda is chosen by the ancestral spirits to inspire a war against the white invaders who have attained a stranglehold on the land of the black inhabitants. Lyrical and evocative like the Abiku spirit world of Ben Okri's Azaro, this novel does not mention Canada even once but like Buchi Emecheta's *Rape of Shavi*, one may read it as an allegory of a people's first encounter with colonialism and a silent statement on the issues of Colour and Race in post-colonial Canada.

To conclude, even though critics like Ayanna Black write in terms of "a Collective African Consciousness" in African-Canadian literature, the reconstruction of Nation in the works of these writers takes divergent expressions and manifestations and the overall impression is one of "ambivalence," which also marks the rubric of most postcolonial writing in the twentieth century, produced from any location that is informed by the dynamics of colonization. The intensity of this ambivalence is determined by the extent to which a writer is able to balance judiciously the twin pulls of remembrance and forgetting. As Homi K. Bhabha puts it, it is the forgetting a minus in the origin, the shedding of the cultural baggage—that constitutes the beginning of the nation's narrative. Again, it is through the syntax of forgetting or being obliged to forget—that the problematic identification of a national people—becomes visible.[15]

To this perhaps a writer like M.G. Vassanji would react: which Nation? India? East Africa? Tanzania? Britain? USA? Canada? and which National People? The boundaries are forever shifting and there are no National People—only generations of wanderers linked occasionally by a "Community" or a shared past—wanderers who travel great distances with no specific anthems on their lips and perhaps multiculturalism in their minds—wanderers who belong to and therefore reconstruct a Nation which is "nowhere and everywhere" at the same time.

NOTES

1 Ernest Renan, "What is a Nation?," trans. Martin Thomas, *Nation and Narration*, ed. Homi K. Bhabha (London and New York: Routledge 1990), p. 19.

2. Ayanna Black, ed., *Voices: Canadian Writers of African Descent* (Toronto: Harper Perennial, 1992), includes Caribbean writers in Canada.

3. Claire Harris, *Poets in Limbo: A Mazing Space, Writing Canadian Women Writing*, ed. Shirly Neuman and Smaro Kamboureli (Edmonton: Longspoon/NeWest Press, 1986), p. 115.

4. Cyril Dabydeen, *Goatsong* (Ottawa: Mosaic, 1977), p. 16.

5. Carmen Rodriguez, "Going Home: Reflections on Issues of Colour, Culture, Gender and Exile," *Colour An Issue*, ed. Roy Miki and Fred Wah Numbers, 13/14, Spring-Fall, 1994, pp. 21-22.

6. Arnold Harrichand Itwaru, *The Intervention of Canada* (Toronto: TSAR, 1990).

7. Arnold Harrichand Itwaru, "Visible Invisibility: The Anguished Other and the Canadian Discourse," *Indian Journal of Canadian Studies*, Vol. V, 1996, p. 102.

8. Reshard Gool, "Introduction," *Medusa's Eye Square* (Charlottetown: Deal Publications, 1972).

9. Uma Parameswaran, *Saclit: An Introduction to South Asian Canadian Literature* (Madras: East-West Books, 1996), p. 164.

10. (Toronto: TSAR, 1992), p. viii.

11. M.G. Vassanji, *Creative Conflicts: Multi Culturalism in the Mind*. Paper presented at the Seminar "Muse and Minorities" at IIC, New Delhi, Sept. 20-22, 1996. Unpublished.

12. List of Anglophone African-Canadian writers: Neil Bissondath (from Trinidad), Dionne Brand (Caribbean), Nourbese Philip (West Indies), Makeda Silvera (West Indies), Molara Ogundipe Lesile (Nigeria), Frederick Ward (U.S.A.), Austin Clarke (Barbados), Afua Cooper (Jamaica), Cecil Foster (Bardados). Nigel Darbasie (Trinidad), Norma De

Haarte (Guyana), Rozena Maart (South Africa), Yasmin Ladha (Tanzania), Ayanna Black (Jamaica), Farid Karodia (South Africa).

13. Iqbal Ian Rashid, *Black Markets White Boy Friends* (Toronto: TSAR, 1991), p. 5.
14. Yvonne Vera, *Nehanda* (Toronto: TSAR, 1994).
15. Homi K Bhabha, "Dissemi Nation: Time, Narrative and the Margins of Modern Nation" in *Nation and Narration*, p. 310.

Moving with the Movement: A Study of the Inputs, Influences and Interpenetrations of the American Movement with the African American Movement as Manifested in Poetry

SARBANI SEN

Black, a primeval, poignant and powerful colour, is by no means an uninteresting, uniform monotone. Just as there are many shades of black, there are many kinds of Black experience.

Blacks all over the world have undergone long centuries of discrimination, degradation and deprivation. It is only in the twentieth century that the Blacks, under a passionate urge for recognition and acceptance, began their quest for real freedom, equality and autonomy. The Negritude movement in Africa and the Afro-American movement in the United States helped the blacks in the two continents to move from subjugation to self-expression, from suppression to assertion, from darkness to light. Though mutually affective and fundamentally alike, the two movements traversed different courses, taking on different challenges and overcoming different hurdles. Contrasting the philosophy and poetry of the leading lights of the two movements would show where they were alike and where different.

The Negritude movement began in the twenties. Originating in the Negrismo movement in Cuba, it passed through the West Indies before reaching Africa. It was a direct reaction to European acculturation and was responsible for awakening Africans to a consciousness of their might and potential. It marked the emergence of an oppressed people into an articulate awareness of their insulted and traumatic history of colonialism. It rejected the imperialist's theory that the African past was dull, null and void. Instead it sought to create a black mystique to help in the decolonization of the African mind. It taught the Africans the value of tradition, legends, myths and folklore. It proclaimed the black man as a man of dance, rhythm and song. "Emotion is Negro," they declared, "as reason is Greek."[1]

In its attempt to reinstil African pride in their history and traditions, the Negritudinist rejected all things Western. The movement itself was born, after all, of the desire of Black people to free themselves from White standards of Western culture. The militant assertion of their independent humanity was natural in a long suffering race who were trying to recover their pride, confidence and identity. Negritude was a defiance hurled at those who had reduced the black to the status of a beast, to recognize him as a man. It taught the African that his ancestor was no Gaule, but a black man like himself, and all the better for it. In Nkosi's words, "It was the African's breastplate against culture that wanted to dominate it."[2]

Leopold Sedar Senghor was one of the prime champions of Negritude. He described Negritude as "the sum total of the values of the African world."[3] It was a complete ensemble of the values of African culture; an exploration of the collective dreams of the African peoples. Belonging to French colonized Senegal, a state in Africa of which he was to become President, Senghor envisaged Negritude as more than a rejection of French assimilation. It was, to Senghor, an assertion of the validity of African ways of thinking and African modes of apprehending reality. It was a championing of the African's "sense of the divine" and "his identification with life or rather the life force."[4] Negritude, to Senghor, was more than an existential philosophy, more than even a way of being and becoming. It was a complete way of living. Senghor emphasized the sense of group and community inherent in the African psyche which makes him a better human being than the individualistic White. Negritude to Senghor was a movement towards self-awareness of the African people.

Senghor's poems written when he was in exile from Africa, breathe nostalgia and longing. Building a poetic career out of loneliness, alienation and the contradictory pulls of Paris and Africa, his poems reveal an ardour for Africa that borders on idolization. No wonder Jean-Paul Sartre described his love for Africa as a feeling for an "imaginary continent."[5] Nevertheless he was unambiguous in his beliefs in African traditional tenets that mark him out as a Negritude poet, even though he wrote originally in French.

Senghor's attitude to death, for one, is distinctly African. Death does not have the European stamp of finality for him. Instead he subscribed to the African belief that the living and the dead are in continuous contact. Like his fellow Africans, Senghor also looked upon ancestors as guardians of morality and believed that they may be reborn. In "Visit," he describes the hour of communion with the dead:

> I dream in the intimate semi-darkness of an afternoon.
> I am visited by the fatigues of the day,
> The deceased of the year, the souvenirs of the decade, . . .
> And suddenly my dead draw near me. . . .

Another example of his rejection of the "Whiteude" is in his advocacy of the African world view and the African idea of a man's relationship with his fellows. In *Nocturnes*, he focuses on the Negro's oneness with the rest of humanity and his union with Nature. Nature, for Senghor, is the African rural environment of his childhood, untouched and undefiled. African musical instruments like flutes, balafong, tama and riti abound in his poems. The Congo river means a lot to an African, and Senghor is no exception:

> Oh! Congo, asleep in your bed of forests
> queen over Africa made subject . . .
> Mother of all things in whose nostrils is breath . . .
> Great woman! Water wide open to the oar and the canoe's stem.

Another important aspect of Senghor's Negritude is the portrayal of the African woman as living embodiment of natural values. The Western woman, unlike her, has "no mother breast," no "tender words for mouths are lipless," and worse, they have "artificial hearts" that have to be bought with "hard cash."[6]

Senghor is not apologetic about his view of the civilized world as he believes it has lost the African's vital link with Nature. Instead, he declares that the West has a lot to learn from Africa. In "New York," he proclaims how black blood can save the world:

> . . . let the black blood flow into your blood
> Clearing the rust from your steel articulations
> like an oil of life
> Giving your bridges the curve of the hills,
> the liana's suppleness.

Senghor wanted his African brethren to preserve their natural virtues. He wanted them to realize that their accepting Western culture would not mean they being accepted as black-skinned Europeans. Hence they should discover their true selves beneath layers of colonial history. While not preaching racism or racial discrimination, Senghor was definitely advocating racial awareness.

Senghor was adept in the French language. He was a master of rhythm and lyricism. But the paradox lies in the fact that he used the French culture, Western logic to reject Western values, leading to the charge that he swung between the poles of assimilation and rejection. How far the charge is true may be understood by comparing him with Langston Hughes of America.

Generations of African-Americans had been victimized and disfavoured by the White majority culture of the United States. A strong movement was necessary to rehabilitate the African-American's ego. Stretching from the late 1920s into the 60s and beyond, the African-American struggle shared the Negritudinist's denial of assimilation. But what differentiates them from their African brothers was that they did not really reject white culture. Though they looked to Africa as their Mother Continent, the African-Americans were actually searching for an identity within the American context and continent. The Afro-American movement, in its early stages at least, helped to restore the lost link between White America and Black America. In Hughes's words,

> I too sing America
> I am the darker brother
> They send me to eat in the kitchen
> When company comes
> But I laugh
> And eat well
> And grow strong.
> Tomorrow,
> I'll sit at the table . . .
> They'll see how beautiful I am
> and be ashamed
> I, too, am America.

In spite of this basic difference, the African-American, like the Negritudinist, believed in "primitive innocence" and glorified the past.

The Afro-American movement not only issued a clarion call to the African-American to take his rightful place in America's destiny, but also wanted the White American to accept, respect and learn from Negro culture. The movement was born of the tension in the African-American's mind over his dual identity. Negro nationalism itself was a natural reflex to the experience of racial rejection. Much like a child, they decided to rebuff the culture that had rebuffed them. Its adherents therefore condemned white culture as corrupt, decaying and dying, while exalting all that is distinctive in Negro life.

For the White American, on the other hand, championing of Negro "naturalness" was a reaction to the increasing mechanization of American life. In a post-Freudian environment, it seemed right to be primitive, instinctive and sexually uninhibited as they fantasized the Negro to be. Again, it also helped them to assuage their guilt over their role in the black American's slave-past. The result on the Black psyche however was that they too began to indulge in fantasizing their past and themselves. As Hughes puts it, the "Negro Vogue" made us "too conscious of ourselves, provided too many easy opportunities for some of us who drink gin to drink more gin."[7]

It was a long time before the Black writer could break out of the stereotype. And Hughes helped in no small way in this effort. He not only corrected the image of Blacks in the White mind but also helped the Blacks to confront the reality of the massive presence of Whites. He moved away from the path of assimilation designed to make every black man a white everyman. In this refusal, literature became his weapon. He interpreted the black world in his works, describing their hopes, fears and anxieties. His poems were a confrontation of reality, not an outpouring of hate and fear. In other words, he did not sacrifice his art to propaganda.

Hughes was a very genuine, lucid, skilful and natural poet. The deep feeling, integrity and personal element in his poems are unmistakable. His poems were often set to music. Hughes attained a manner of cultivated artlessness, all the more remarkable because he wrote of ethnic peculiarities and tensions. No wonder, he was considered the star extraordinaire of the Harlem Renaissance galaxy of intellects.

Hughes was described as the "Harlem Shakespeare."[8] He was regarded as "the cultural ambassador of his race in the court of world opinion." (73) A prolific poet, he had a deep love for his people like Senghor. He once said, "I never tire of hearing the talk of the gayest and bravest people possible facing tremendous odds, working, laughing and trying to get somewhere in the world." (73) More than anyone else, he articulated the concept of American Negritude, helping new writers to come into their own both at home and abroad.

Hughes incorporated cultural folk rhythms, worksongs, vernacular jokes and blues into his poems. He portrayed the archetypal black who hears the Euphrates or the Congo rhythm in his blood in "The Negro Speaks of Rivers":

> I've known rivers
> I've known rivers ancient as the world and older than the flow of
> blood in human veins.
> My soul has grown deep like the rivers.
> I bathed in the Euphrates when dawns were young.
> I built my hut near the Congo and it lulled me to sleep.
> I looked upon the Nile and raised the pyramids above it. . . .
> I've known rivers
> Ancient, dusky rivers
> My soul has grown deep like rivers.

Hughes had a greater sense of music than Senghor. A simple poet, he wrote his poems in a spirit of jazz. His "Blues" poems became the rage. But the paradox about these poems as Hughes himself points out is that the mood of the Blues is almost always despondent but when they are sung, people laugh.

Hughes had a boundless zest for life, an irrepressible humour and an undeniable versatility. While there was an element of protest in his poetry, he always wanted to be considered a poet, without the implication of race. The fact that he was only half-Negro gave him the critical distance that is essential for good poetry. Though African meant a great deal to him, he took it with a sense of fun. He was no primitivist. That is why he rejected his patroness who wanted him to be just that. His remark on this matter indicates his attitude and temperament. He said:

> She wanted me to be primitive and know and feel the intuitions of the primitive. But unfortunately, I did not feel the rhythms of the primitive surging through me. . . . I was only an American Negro—who had loved the surface of Africa and the rhythms of Africa—but I was not Africa. . . . And I was not what she wanted me to be.[9]

Though a stalwart of the Harlem Renaissance, he did not aim at division as much as integration on equal terms. He wanted the African-Americans to realize that they could not be separated from America. The Negritude movement in Africa, on the other hand, was more militant and could be described as "anti-racist racism." Though both movements aimed at a vindication of Black pride, the African movement was more aggressive, rhetorical and political. An outstanding feature of the black movement writers on both sides of the continent was their incorporation of African rhythms and tones into their verse, beginning thereby a new chapter in English poetry.

The inherent danger of the movements lay in their tendency to indulge in negro-narcissisms. The exaltation of the Negro persona scaled to dizzy heights in Negritude poetry till Neo-Negritudinists like Wole Soyinka appeared on the scene to correct the distortion. No longer were they ready to indulge in a collective neurosis. "Negritude appeared to them," as Ousmane puts it, "to have nothing solid about it." (Nkosi, 15) He points out how "those who preach Negritude are often most closely allied with those who profit most from African backwardness." (15) Negritude thus became an aspect of neo-colonialism. There was the realization that African culture did not really need props to hold it up. Negritude, as it existed, could only lead to a blind alley. It was also no longer psychologically or politically necessary in postcolonial Africa. After all, Negritude could not feed the hungry or build roads.

Writers like Soyinka helped their brethren to proceed beyond Negritude. They taught their people to view their past with realism, neither glamorizing nor deprecating it. As Soyinka puts it, "A tiger does not proclaim his tigritude, he pounces." (Feuser, 204) He agreed with Mphahlele that "Negritude was another aspect of the autocolonization of Africa," (208) "an intellectual pastime of the governing elite." (209)

Akinwande Oluwole Soyinka was not going to allow his people to continue to cry over spilt milk. He spearheaded the movement of restoring restraint to African life and letters. For his brave stand, he was condemned as "the apocalyptic villain, in an imperialist commando raid." (204) He was condemned for wasting a "generation of opportunities for cultural liberation." (204) Undaunted, Soyinka stuck to his guns. In his plays and poems, he courageously portrayed African life as it really was.

Wole Soyinka, Nobel Laureate, is a prolific poet. His poetry has a well-organized system of images, a sensitivity to landscape and intimations of deeper meanings. In all his collected poems—*Idanre, A Shuttle in the Crypt, Poems from Prison, Ogun Abibiman*—there is a critical control that lends the poems greater power.

The poems of the road capture the reality of death. Death on the road is a kind of self-sacrifice to progress. Another image that predominates in his poems is that of the loner. The dreamer and the loner walk the solitary path in his poems to martyrdom for the welfare of society. His poems have very obviously an African origin. He has written numerous poems about African myths and legends. For example, Ogun, the Yoruban God of destruction and creation has great significance for Soyinka because of his ambivalent nature. The legend of Ogun is used in *Idanre* and *Ogun Abibiman,* allowing the poet to introduce various themes like war, death and free will. Since Soyinka is himself attempting to create a meaning out of the contradictory forces governing human life, Ogun is for him an apt symbol.

Soyinka is actually concerned with the problems of postcolonial Nigeria. He has written numerous poems on contemporary events as he has written some on personal experiences. Though Soyinka is a serious poet, a Nature-poet, he can also be ironic, witty, youthful and charmingly playful. One of the poems he wrote in prison, where he found himself for his uncompromising honesty, sparkles with Soyinka's sense of fun. The poem "Telephone Conversation" is remarkably free from any bitterness, hatred or anger, though it deals with inter-race relationship:

> The price seemed reasonable, location indifferent. The landlady swore she lived off premises. Nothing remained but self-confession: "Madam," I warned, "I hate a wasted journey—I am African."
> Silence. Silenced transmission of pressurized good breeding. . . .
> "HOW DARK?" . . . I had not misheard. . . ."ARE YOU LIGHT OR VERY DARK?" Button B. Button A. Stench.
> . . . It was real! Shamed
> By ill-mannered silence, surrender
> Pushed dumbfoundment to beg simplification
> Considerate, she was, varying the emphasis—
> "ARE YOU DARK? OR VERY LIGHT?" Revelation came.
> "You mean—like plain or milk chocolate?"
> Her assent was clinical. . . .
> I chose. "West African Sepia" . . .
> . . . "WHAT'S THAT?" conceding
> "DON'T KNOW WHAT THAT IS." "Like brunette."
> "THAT'S DARK ISN'T IT?" "Not altogether."
> Facially, I am brunette, but madam, you should see
> The rest of me. Palm of my hand, soles of my feet

Are a peroxide blonde. Friction caused—
Foolishly madam—by sitting down, has turned
My bottom raven black—One moment madam!
                                        sensing—
Her receiver rearing on the thunderclap
About my ears—"Madam," I pleaded,
                              "wouldn't you rather
see for yourself?"

The poem is indicative of how the Negritude movement and African poets were acquiring balance, restraint and self-control. The American case on the other hand was very different.

The Afro-American movement became radical and revolutionary under the impact of political events in the sixties. The emergence of Martin Luther King and his "direct action" struggle against racial segregation in buses and schools set the Black imagination on fire. The discovery of the heroism they were capable of and the realization that "Black was beautiful" made the Black American more confident and assertive. The political manifestation of this mood was the "Black Power" movement while its cultural and literary arm was the "Black Aesthetic" movement. Among the protagonists of this new school of artists was LeRoi Jones. With him, a new kind of poetry came into being. Bearing the communal stamp of Black brotherhood, his poems were more elemental, fiery and dedicated to a Black Ideal than his predecessors. LeRoi Jones wrote:

> The Black Artist's role in America is to aid in the destruction of America as he knows it. His role is to report and reflect so precisely the nature of the society, and of himself in that society, that other men will be moved by the exactness of his rendering and, if they are blackmen, grow strong through this moving, having seen their own strength, and weakness; and if they are white men, tremble, curse and go mad, because they will be drenched by the filth of their evil.[10]

The black writer was to be the conscience-keeper of the country. He was to address his people directly, identifying completely with them. If Harlem had been the Mecca of the earlier group of poets, New York, which they renamed "New Ark," became the centre of intense black activity now. And LeRoi Jones was the centre of this new Black movement.

LeRoi Jones wanted a reordering of aesthetics in order that poetry could incorporate Black symbolism, mythology and iconology. His association with the Beats and Olson and his reading of Williams and Stevens left their mark on his poems. He underwent a Zen and Yoruban phase before he became a Muslim and adopted the Arabic name, Imamu Amiri Baraka, abandoning the slave name LeRoi Jones.

Imamu Amiri Baraka declared about his poems: "How You sound is what we recent fellows are up to. . . . My poetry is whatever I think I am."[11] This is how he described himself in one of his poems:

> I'm Evett LeRoi Jones, 30 years old
> A black nigger in the universe. A long breath singer
> Would-be dancer, strong from years of fantasy
> And study . . .
> I am a meditative man. . . . My heart is large as my mind
> this is a messenger calling, over here—open your eye.
> And your ears and your souls, today is the history we must learn
> to discover. There is no guilt in love.

He can also be sarcastic, as in the following:

> Luxury, then, is a way of
> being ignorant, comfortably
> . . . where theories
> can thrive, under heavy tarpaulins
> Without being cracked by ideas.

Baraka's poems are always energetic, existential, open and blatant. In *The Dead Lectures* and *Black Art*, his anger at racial discrimination gives his poems a strange intensity. *Blue People* and *Blue Music* on the other hand reveal Baraka as a connoisseur of jazz.

All of Baraka's poems reveal his disillusionment with White culture which reached its peak with the assassination of Martin Luther King in 1968. He did not believe in the artistic theory of poetry; subscribing instead to the belief that like all human activity, poetry is also political. His poems were racy, revolutionary and interesting and helped Afro-Americans to find their moorings in a multi-racial society. A prolific writer, he published numerous plays as well as poems.

Baraka's use of Black speech rhythms and traditions makes him a poet who more than anyone else, realized Black potential. He represented the best of the Black Aesthetic movement. His kind of poetry became the ideal of Black poets of the sixties. In Ron Karenga's words: "Black art must expose the enemy, praise the people and support the revolution. It must be like LeRoi Jones's poems that are assassin's poems, poems that kill and shoot guns and wrassle cops into alleys taking their weapons leaving them dead with tongues pulled out." (Scott 307) Though his vitality and power is unmistakable, he lacks the critical distance that characterizes a Soyinka. This failing is common to all Black Aesthetic writers and critics who consider it blasphemy that black literature aspire to be universal, rather than restrictive.

The Black movement in America, unlike its African counterpart, is yet to emerge from the envenomed prisonhouse of race. The Black Aesthetic movement radicalized the ethics of the Harlem Renaissance writers, while the Neo-Negritudinists had softened the philosophy of their predecessors. Though the two movements had moved in opposite directions and evolved differently largely due to the impulse of political events, they remained fundamentally alike and philosophically similar. Both movements aimed at

1. The creation of racial pride and the assertion of race consciousness
2. The forging of a new approach to White institutions and values
3. Glorification of past history
4. Retention of primitive innocence
5. Championing of "Black is Beautiful"
6. Rebellion against cultural domination
7. The emergence of a new Negro

The significance of the movements to Blacks all over the world was momentous. It awakened their latent power and potential and made them realize that they had to have something to teach the world. The Whites on the other hand had to learn to accept that their myths had failed. There was no "Whiteman's burden" in Africa, just as "the American Dream" was just that, a dream. By forcing both the Blacks and Whites to confront the truth, the movements were, in effect making mutual understanding and friendship possible.

The movements had tremendous importance for literature as well. They had made a whole new kind of poetry possible. What is additionally significant is that the Movement writers had rejuvenated a tired language by incorporating African tones, sounds and rhythms into it. They had vitalized the English language and what's better, they had extracted a forgotten, buried music from it. But what is perhaps of the greatest consequence is that the Movements had proved that literature, even in the post-modern world, can be confident, assured and meaningful. And in this lies their supreme, universal significance.

NOTES

1. Eldred D. Jones, *The Writing of Wole Soyinka* (London: Heinemann, 1973), p. 9.
2. Lewis Nkosi, *Tasks and Masks: Themes and Styles of African Literature* (1981), p. 15.
3. Willfried F. Feuser, "Wole Soyinka: The Problem of Authenticity," *The Literary Half Yearly*, 28:2 (1987), p. 205.
4. Abiola Irele, "Negritude: Literature and Ideology," *Modern Black Novelists: A Collection of Critical Essays*, ed. Robert Bone (Englewood Cliffs, New Jersey: Prentice Hall, 1971), p. 19.
5. Gerald Moore, "Introduction," *Seven African Writers*, p. xix.
6. Leopold Senghor, "New York" (Poem).
7. Amritjit Singh, "Black-White Symbiosis," *Studies in American Literature* (1976), p. 34.
8. Usha Shourie, "Langston Hughes," *The Black American Literature* (1985), p. 73.
9. Ezekiel Mphahlele, "Langston Hughes," *Introduction to African Literature: An Anthology of Critical Writing*, ed. Ulli Beier (Harlow: Longman, 1982), p. 82.
10. Nathan A. Scott, Jr., "Black Literature," *Harvard Guide to Contemporary American Writing*, ed. Daniel Hoffman (New Delhi: OUP, 1979), p. 307.
11. Ihab Hassan, ed., "Introduction," *Contemporary American Literature* (New York: Frederick Ungar, 1973), p. 136.

Nigerian Gender Poetry

PAUL O IHEAKARAM

Poetry is man and of course woman.

Niyi Osundare

Poetry, as imaginative literature, is one of humankind's most compressed forms of communication. Even in its concise nature, it obeys the law of gender. Gender poetry is at least twelve centuries old if we take *Beowulf* as the work of a Christian poet of the eighth century. The major characters in that poem are male (Beowulf and Grendel) and female (Grendel's mother, a water-hag). In the first-half of the twelfth century, Courtly love ideas dominated Medieval Romance and in the fourteenth century, Petrarch's 'Laura love poems'[1] consolidated love-poetry (usually in the form of pleas and complaints) in favour of the female gender because under the convention the male character addresses his love poems and songs to his lady. Petrarchan love doctrines subsequently influenced English lyrics and set the standard and moral for Renaissance and Elizabethan love sonnet-sequences.[2] In American poetry, Walt Whitman's mid-nineteenth century *Leaves of Grass* (1855) is a celebration of gender; especially "Song of Myself" is a poem of endurance and masculinity. In African poetry, the popular "practitioner" of the love-poetry convention, only in the limited sense of addressing a female character in Lyrics, is Dennis Brutus (*Letters to Martha*) 1969 in his rather peculiar circumstances. In male gender poetry, his "Troubadour" comes easily to my mind too.

Nigerian gender poetry does not pattern its form or content on the love-poems of English lyrics of the Elizabethans or post-Elizabethans. Rather male and female characters in Nigerian poetry are merely incidental to the poet's subject matter or theme which is usually not love. Nigerian gender poems are, therefore, not "love-poems" in the real sense of the term since they lack feminine and "masculine persuasive force" (to borrow from Donne) characteristic of Renaissance and some Metaphysical verse.

Ukwu I. Ukwu's poem, "A Bus Ride,"[3] for instance, captures a fast moving panorama appropriate in a bus journey where the passengers include familiar and strange characters on long and short bus ride. There are "Two ample women" who "discuss their friends for all the world to hear"; there is a man "lost in his *Daily Times*"; there is "a gallant" and fop who says "'My dear' to a strange girl, who glares at him"; there is a tramp and, of course, there is "the bus conductor." Male and female genders are fully represented as well as their generation differences: two women, a man, a boy and a girl. Their presence in the poem is to force the attention of the reader on the different interests, moods, actions and reactions of people gathered in a small space; and to the rush, the confusion, the babel and the hubbub in the situations presented. The effect is that the reader is a conscious observer of the behaviour of the characters in the poem.

Mable Segun is one of Nigeria's pioneer female poets. Her piece "The Pigeon-Hole" is a female gender poem. But again, the woman's situation (her problems with "a delinquent child") is the central concern of the poem:

> waiting in constant fear,
> listening for the dreaded knock
> and the cold tones of policeman:
> 'Madam; you're wanted at the station'
> she used to say,
> 'It's the uncertainty that worries me
> if only I know for certain.[4]

Christopher Okigbo's poems in *Labyrinths* are very strong male gender presentations; as strong, one would say, as Whitman's "Song of Myself." Here is Whitman proclaiming his manhood: "who touches this touches a man." And Okigbo, in the same number of words, "watchman for the watchword at Heavensgate." ("Heavensgate: The Passage"), or in their exhibition of sexual enjoyment: "An American, one of roughs, a kosmos, disorderly fleshy and sensual . . .. eating and drinking and breeding." And Okigbo: "I have had my cleansing,/ Emigrant with airborne nose./ The he-goat-on-heat." ("Limits: Siren Limits") Other African male motifs and imageries in Okigbo's poems include: drums, canons, masks, thunder, hunters, town-crier, bayonets and rams. In Okigbo's poetry the male/hero is symbolized by the sunbird. The Watermaid represents the female character, the lioness. She has an ambivalent quality—gentle and harmless, "my lioness" silent sister; destructive—she destroys the hero's second self.

The brief appearance of a female character, the "Watermaid" in "Heavensgate" is at the invocation of the male protagonist as part of his initiation rites:

> Bright
> with the armpit-dazzle of a lioness,
> she answers,
> wearing white light about her,
> and the waves escort her,
> my lioness,
> crowned with moonlight.
> So brief her presence.[5]

The next, but longer female presence is an imagery in "Silences" where, in "Lament of the Silent Sisters," "the image of drowning virgins, and the dream of ultimate martyrdom are present." (11)

When the female character (the lioness) appears again in "Limits IV," she "destroys the hero's second self." Unlike the female characters in "Laments of the Silent Sisters," she is not an image; she is real and physically present before the hero. But she is an evil force which the Sisters are not. Her "image insists . . ./ Her image distracts/ With the cruelty of the rose . . ./ Oblong-beaded lioness—/ No shield is proof against her." Even the fragrance from her armpit "turns chloroform" which suggests death for the hero. In "Limits V" she is referred to be a beast and she kills the hero, "the Sunbird," in "Limits X"; a re-enactment of the death of the hero's second self in "Limits IV." But "The sunbird sings again," that is, survives "Where the caress (of the lioness) does not reach" ("Limits XII"); which proves the hero as made "From frame of iron,/And in mould of iron." ("Limits VII") Although the hero, the sunbird, survives in "Limits," he does foreshadow his death in "Heavensgate" as "the spirit in the ascent"; and in his "swan song" of "Silences III." He is then finally killed (symbolically in battle) in "Path of Thunder" (not by the female character) where "The glimpse of a dream lies in a cave,/ together with the mortally wounded birds." In all, female characters in Okigbo's poetry are weaker than the male character whose masculine activities (initiation rites, town-crying, drumming, hunting and warfare) make not only stronger but dominant gender.

Ifeyinwa Lekwa is a gender poetess. Two of her Collections attest to this. She has obtrusive interest in women and young girls especially in their attraction to the exploitation by men. Her tone of suspicion of men rings infinitely in her gender poems. Part 4 of her *Shadows and Reflections,*[6] titled "Women's World" has nine poems. In their escapism and eroticism they regret (she uses the world "Lament") the fate of women as wives and mothers. Women see themselves as victims and see men as exploiters of their resources. The poems are anti-men in their female voices of protest. In her male gender poems ("Understanding Him" and "Unhurried Wait for Him"), men are presented as causers of pain, doubt and sorrow; of panic, turbulence and upheaval for women. "Bridal Night" and "Teats of Solace," from her *Bountiful Harvests,*[7] are concealed female and male gender poems consumed by sensual imagery and (unlike the gender poems in *Shadows*) the woman desires and invites the man to convulsive and passionate sexual session:

Come into me
Pierce . . .
a virgin cry
may throbbing spears
quench mid-night flames
descend to my valley
trespass my island
dive deep to
precious pearls

And "in the heat/ of the moment/ the man sucked" the "erect nipples" of youthful breasts.

Niyi Osundare's poem, "Search for a Wife"[8] involves male and female characters in action and words. At thirty, Idowu's (the male character's) purpose for searching for a wife is to have "somebody to lay one's food/on the table, decked with/beautiful antimacassar"; a selfish motive, one might say. But the beauty of the poem lies in its conceit embedded in the mode of communication among the characters and with the reader. Idowu interacts directly with "his mother-in-law to be" and with his mother. But Idowu's mother, his mother-in-law and the reader communicate indirectly:

". . . the fault is not the hunchback's
but that of his hunch: yōur mother
is a great curser"

"I went visiting a young woman
today, mother, but her mother vows
her daughter will never be wife
to a curser's child"
"Whoever says I am a curser,
may he see his own ears
without a mirror, may *Soponna*
turn his house into a furnace,
may Sango. . . . "

The poem ends like a riddle session where two genders (male and female) are gathered in a moonlit night to search for the answer to the question: "Is Idowu's mother a curser or not?" Again, like many Nigerian gender poems, the interest is not in the male and female characters as such but in their actions, attitudes and views.

Osundare's "Bride's Song"[9] is a female gender poem; in some respects like Lekwa's "Bridal Night" and in other respects unlike her "Woman's World" poems. Osundare's bride is eager and happy to go to her husband's house and to play the role of a wife and mother:

I go now
And the moon is witness to my leaving
Before this moon hears the first cock
My belly will be round
Like grandmother's laden bowl

Marriage is a pleasure to the bride and the excitement of proving her virginity to her husband overwhelms her:

Tell husband's mother
I will take a full-throated cock
When the first night's sheet glows
With the virtue of many years

Osundare, the male poet, is gentle and appreciative of female characters while Lekwa, the poetess, is hostile to male, and even to female, characters. "This indicates an obvious assumption that men understand women's issues better than women."[10]

In Catherine Obianuju Acholonu's *Nigeria in the Year 1999* (1985), four poems have definite gender characters. "Other Forms of Slaughter" is of female gender and presents "innocent virgins" who are victims of the immorality of war. The poetess captures in very vivid language of violence the force with which young girls were made to surrender their maidenhead by soldiers of the victorious side of the Nigeria-Biafra war. It was "a lustful era of anarchic bestiality."

> When hands of sandpaper
> jar at tender tendons of daughter drums
> when rods of aggression rip through sealed valves
> of flutes of reed when heaving chests pin
> them down
> then greedy hands
> rummaging
> tear open
> the frills of their delicate legend[11]

Although this is a female gender poem, it shows the cruel, savage and disgusting side of man. In this extension, the poem can be seen as a male and female gender poem. It, therefore, agrees with the image of man (in Ifeyinwa Lekwa's poem) as an exploiter and woman as his victim.

In the next female gender poem, "The Dissidents," Acholonu's character is "the daughter of my father"; a benevolent peacemaker:

> She gave out white chalk
> and they painted their toes she gave out kola-nuts
> and together they ate to appease the angry earth

The 'daughter of my father' also has supernatural powers; "she lifted her arm/ and like lightning/ quelled the storm." She brings the blessings of rain. But her powers are superceded by those of *Amadioha*, a male character; a god of thunder:

> *amadioha* struck
> lashing black fire on the dissidents
> earth sucked their blood and all was still.

The mediating and transforming power of "the daughter of my father" does not change the dissidents and so they perish. In the two poems, the male characters play violent roles and the female ones are either innocent victims of masculine force or peacemakers.

The "Water Woman" (she is "Watermaid" in Okigbo) is a female gender poem without the overt participation of a male character. The water woman has a number of praise names which make the poem to take the form of an incantation; addressing the water woman as

> owner of the drink of life
> beauty that blinds the eye
> source of all woman's vice
> fire that burns in water

The "blinding beauty" and shape of the water woman is alluring to the male character:

> Beauty that blinds the eye
> that breeds the insatiable thirst
> in man's bossom
> slimy
> tender source of all woman's vice

The water woman has a magnetic force; her "wish is law" to whoever she wants to take to her abode, "the sea's bottom." Her victim "must hurry and follow." The poetess paints for us a chilling picture of the water woman's, the "mother snake's spectral majesty:

> sitting on a throne of snakes
> the sacred python
> round her uplifted arms discarded lifeless figures
> skeletons hooked onto mangrove roots.

This sketch, drawn from popular imagination, adds to the weirdness of her presence. The male figure here is a peripheral character. But it is significant that because he is, in reverse situation, the victim of the female character; she "breeds the insatiable thirst in a man's bosom."

"Embryonic Bride" is a gender poem of two male and one female characters. It is a poem of revenge. The protagonist is the male counterpart of the water woman. He swears the destruction of his rival male lover and his "faithless bride." The fiendish bridegroom has diabolic powers from the sea to which he belongs:

> . . . I will trash him
> with the force of the waves and feed the scorpions
> with his prick
> then his eyes will crack as kola
> between the teeth of him
> that controls the waters.

The male victim's offence to the "water man" is that while he waited for the bride's "day of maturity" and

> hoping to taste your first up
> wine
> he stole into your attending chamber
> and planting himself between your legs
> drank the wine and broke the pot

For this audacity the bridegroom threatens:

> only by sucking his blood
> from his veins
> shall I hope to find redress
> I will break the calabash of his head
> on the rocks at the sea bottom.

And for the faithless bride,

> you shall be offered to me
> on the altar of the sea and with the weeds clinging
> to your naked skin I will consummate our defiled marriage
> and when my lust is alleviated
> I shall throw you to the crabs

The bridegroom in "Embryonic Bride" and the water woman in the poem of that title are malignant supernatural creatures. The ritual language in both poems evokes an atmosphere of horror in a vision like in S.T. Coleridge's "Christabel."

Two factual points emerge from our consideration of Acholonu's gender poetry. She is fascinated by the relationship, of whatever kind, between supernatural creatures and human beings. She appears to see the relationship as normal and inevitable and as similar to the line between ancestors and the living in Igbo world view. She reflects the complementarity of opposites (male and female for example) that exists in nature. Each of her gender poems involves male and female characters even if either plays a minor role. Consequently, no matter how romantic the world of her male or female poems is, the natural phenomenon in the co-existence of the opposite sexes makes it somewhat realistic.

Considering the large corpus of Nigerian poetry, our gender poetry is scanty and the number of Nigerian female poets is also small compared with their male counterparts. The paucity of gender poetry is perhaps attributable to lack of romantic writing in our contemporary literature. Our literature is still shy about love. We do not have "love poems" because our idea of love is culturally conditioned. We see love as a private affair which does not need to be spoken or written about for public consumption. This cultural attitude has denied our literature the expression of deep feelings and thoughts that love brings about. It is rather in pop-music/songs that this cultural inhibition has been shelved. What is not of public interest is yet to be considered worthy of our poetry. This is why politics, corruption, fraud and other social issues are favoured subjects for poetry and love is not. Our literature is still relatively new and may be said to be at its prudery or Victorian stage from which it will mature into making all subjects its province. What Cyprian Ekwensi did with the male and female gender (taking love to the market place) in *Jagua Nana* (1961) has not been repeated by either another Nigerian novelist or poet.

NOTES

1. Francesco Petrarce (1304-1374).
2. See for example, Sir Thomas Wyatt, *Songs and Lyrics* (1557); Sir Philip Sidney, *Astrophel and Stella* (1581); Edmund Spenser, *Amoretti* (1595) and Shakespeare, *Sonnets* (1593-96).
3. John Reed and Clive Wake, ed., *A Book of African Verse* (London: Heinemann, 1964), pp. 82-83.
4. Frances Ademola, ed., *Reflections Nigerian Prose and Verse* (Lagos: African Universities Press, 1962), p. 64.
5. Christopher Okigbo, *Labyrinths* (London: Heinemann, 1971), p. 11.
6. *Shadows and Reflections* (1st Edition, 1986).
7. *Bountiful Harvests* (Owerri: Imo Library Board, 1988).
8. Niyi Osundare, *Village Voices* (Ibadan: Evans Nigeria, 1984), p. 18.

9. *Ibid.*, pp. 41-42.
10. Cyra McFadden, "In Defense of Gender," Paul Escholz et al, ed., *Language Awareness* (New York: St. Martin's Press, 1986), p. 329.
11. Catherine Obianuju Acholonu, *Nigeria in the Year 1999* (Owerri: Totan Publishers, 1985), pp. 32-33.

This article was presented as a paper at the 6th Annual Conference of the West African Association for Commonwealth Literature and Language Studies (WAACLALS), 13-16 April 1994 at Alvan Ikoku College of Education, Owerri Imo State, Nigeria.

The Okigbo Music: A Study of "Distances"

CURWEN BEST

The artistic quest into the realm of religious experience must hold some significance beyond the mere representation of an experience for its own sake. Okigbo's claim of not being sure about the meaning which much of his work conveys beyond the fact of the experience, is nothing new in the domain of the arts, and of literature, in particular. Many writers have from time to time claimed to be oblivious of the 'truth' within their work. Baudelaire readily comes to mind. The Spanish poet Frederico Garcia Lorca has claimed that he writes under the total inspiration of 'dark/black' muse: 'Duende.' Lorca's influence on Okigbo and their relatedness, is merely alluded to within criticism on Okigbo.[1] They share more similarities than are generally acknowledged. Later in this paper I will highlight some of these similarities, as a way of better interpreting the purpose (hidden or otherwise) of Okigbo's continuing quest within "Distances."

It should be stated that whereas "Heavensgate" and "Limits" are predominantly about the spiritual experience of a precarious entrant, "Distances" presents the maturing philosophy and style of and individual mind in its metaphysical workings, under the influence of a medically induced drug. Anaesthesia is however not the central thing here. It is merely a 'physical' inducement which once gave birth to a type of spiritual experience, quite like that achieved through a religious ceremony. The experience of "Distances" is an extension of that experience explored earlier in "Heavensgate," in that many of the motifs are still present. Ultimately, the major concern of "Distances" shifts away from a thematic concern with religious, socio-historical and cultural problems, and focuses on the process of artistic affectation. "Distances" is less directly religious and less spontaneous from its inception.

In "Heavensgate" and "Limits" one's attention is almost always focused on the muse. We find a similar fascination with higher creative power in the Afro-Caribbean poet like Kamau Brathwaite. His sea loa in

Sun Poem introduces his poem's insistence on the higher creative power as critical to self-empowerment. Okigbo assumes the same focus throughout the early sections of *Labyrinths*, in order to define God and Man as the principal actors within his discourse,—thereby calling attention to this thematic imperative. Whereas the external force is the prime source of inspiration and power in the foregoing sections, "Distances" is much more of an introspection. "Distances" is a journey into the self, a process only predicated in "Heavensgate," but not significantly and meaningfully undertaken until "Distances."

In his essay "Okigbo's 'Distances': A Retreat from Christ to Idoto," R.N. Egudu shows reservations about prominent critical approaches which tend to emphasize "not a spiritual but an artistic quest in 'Distances.'" He himself seems to prefer to see it the other way, that is, to see "Heavensgate" and "Limits" as an artistic quest, and "Distances" as a spiritual one. There can be much danger in attempting to bracket the text in the manner. It might require a perspective which is privy to much more information than Okigbo has communicated in life, and much more than now remains, to prescribe the 'true' interpretation of his quest(s) throughout *Labyrinths*. One can be sure that it is equally possible to associate either the spiritual or artistic quest to the 'separate' undertakings, or one to both, or both to each. The critic might feel it his duty either to uphold the more literal approach which sees it all as the proverbial religious rite, or, one might see the religious ritual as a metaphor. In any case some credit should be given the poet for creating these insatiable possibilities.

When Okigbo revealed that his "Heavensgate" is a contribution to his oft-neglected responsibilities of 'carrying on the various periodic rites which were connected with the worship of [Idoto],'[2] this is the closest we might come to labelling his quests. It is from here that one can begin to take on a tentative labelling of his quests. *Labyrinths* is one sustained poem, and the spiritual quest runs through the entire work. However, the spiritual/religious undertaking of "Heavensgate" and "Limits" soon gives way to another concern with the inner workings of the individual('s) soul, and with the process of communicating these innate developments.

For Lorca, the encounter with his muse 'Duende' could not be totally rewarding unless that experience could show some overt effect within his writing (and it does). Much of the insight which his work revealed (e.g. *El Romancero Gitano*) especially with regard to his symbolic portrayal of discriminated gypsies, was due to the inspiration of his muse. So the muse appears only as a catalyst, the means to an end. In a similar way, Okigbo's experience under general anaesthesia is a catalyst to his larger concern of defining and coming to grips with his new found spirituality. This manifests itself through a more conscious preoccupation with form in "Distances." What is distinctly unique about this segment is its ever audible strains of music which accompanies this most unique of inductions. So now, the onus is on the reader to make full sense of these melodies of which we generally know little, but which are the only guide to gauging the effects of this artistic undertaking. Okigbo's music is one of inward voicings:

> From flesh into phantom on the horizontal stone
> I was the sole witness to my homecoming . . .
> For in the inflorescence of the white chamber,
> a voice, from very far away,
> chanted, and the chamber descanted,
> the birthday of earth,
> paddled me home through some dark labyrinth,
> from laughter to the dream. (53)

These inner voices are contrasted with an outer silence, of which Okigbo seeks to make sense:

> But what does my divine rejoicing hold?
> A bowl of incense, a nest of fireflies? (53)

Can he, how can he outwardly verbalize these inner melodies? What language, indeed what kind of language can he employ to communicate the truths of his experience, that it maintains some measure of sense, 'real-ity' and relevance. In an essay on "Distances: Fantasy or Dialectic," Anozie is not prepared to monitor the extent of the 'metaphysical fantasies' within Okigbo's work, since he believes about poetry "that if it is worth anything as art at all any poem ought to have it in itself to disclose and also communicate using its own authentic system of linguistic symbols, . . . A poem is not a metaphysical fantasy. It is a form of human communication." (132-33) One senses that Anozie is firstly speaking at the conventional level of the written word on page. He decries poems like Okigbo's "Distances" which seek to vicariously communicate the sentiments of a metaphysical experience. Yet in his approach to the symbolic word in Okigbo's "Distances," Anozie's method tends to further problematize the already abstruse poem. He engages in:

P = D1 + D2
a = D3 + D4 + D5
r = D6 (146)

The riddle of Okigbo's music cannot achieve its fuller interpretation through this 'scientific' analysis and expression. As the ongoing spiritual experience grows increasingly introspective, it takes him further into a world which places little confidence in the word. The signifier and the signified become disparate entities. In "Distances" the word becomes replaced by sound (and the song) as the most significant and functional symbol of communication. Thus, from a critical perspective, theme is replaced by form, technique, the allusion, and symbolism as the prime source of concern in the work. This is what Okigbo was alluding to when he spoke of it being possible to communicate meaning other than through the intellect.

The entire movement of "Distances" resounds with conflicting melodies. For example, there is the intrusive uncomfortable laughter which breaks the introspective mood of "Distances I." And "Distances V" is a symphony of interchanges between the 'effervescent' utterance, and 'silence.' The result of such arrangement is that they create verse whose mood borders on crazed hysteria. The poet works and reworks this compositional structure of verse (with notes and rests)[3] and this technique takes shape to reemphasize emotional incoherence as an accompaniment to the spiritual/artistic process. In "Distances V" the initiate has not yet fully understood the work which is going on within his soul ('the question in the inkwell'), and neither can he control the movement of conflicting forces about him. So the fifth opus must reflect a type of emotional antagonism, and contradiction through its laughter/silence song play:

each step is the step of the mule in the abyss—
the archway the oval the panel oblong
to that sanctuary of the earth's molten bowel
for the music woven into the funerary rose
the water in the tunnel its effervescent laughter
the open laughter of the grape or vine
the question in the inkwell the answer on the monocle
the unanswerable question in the tabernacle's silence. (58)

In *West African Poetry*, Fraser seems foremost to hear 'a song of hope and rejoicing'[4] in "Distances." But far from that optimism, Okigbo has heightened the nexus of emotional insecurity through a more direct method of counterpointing antithetical conditions and states: from 'Flesh into Phantom' in "Distances I," to the assemblage of contrasting forms/shapes in "Distances IV":

> And at the archway
> a triangular lintel
> of solid alabaster
> enclosed in a square
> inscribed in a circle . . . (57)

For Egudu this meshing of signs 'echoes the words of the Bible' and also 'mocks at the ideals they are meant to symbolize.' He is partially correct, although they are not so much a conscious attempt at parody as they are an apparent symbol of a present disorder, and soon coming new order. Since the process being undergone is not a bona fide anything, it seems to be attempting to assume/inscribe some universal symbol, one which at present appears to have no definite shape, and seems to have even less of spiritual significance, 'with a hollow centre.'

The contrasting voices of "Distances" might also be said to give this movement variation of vocal texture. On three distinct occasions one hears the voice of what must be the God figure. These utterances are italicized. In the first instance ("Distances IV") the tone of this voice is distinct from that which is first introduced within the poem. Much like solo voice it is salient, audacious, and it seeks to give fuller meaning to the preceding, and subsequent utterances. After the description of the enigmatic symbol 'at the archway,' comes the soloist:

> the only way to go
> through the marble archway
> to the catatonic pingpong
> of the evanescent halo . . . (57)

Somehow though, Okigbo does not appear to be the composer who gives too much away. The voice of his soloist, though noticeably distinct in approach and air, is so integrally fused within the work that even though it explains some of the complexities, it still sustains the general sense of mystique introduced with the initial voicings. And then again, on other occasions Okigbo's soloist might (like the chamber of "Distances I") become more dynamically involved within the total composition, by attempting an harmonic range of association. In "Distances I" it is the shrill voice of the descant. In "Distances IV" the soloist voice is shifted from its accustomed straightforward purpose of lucid restatement to conclude this segment with an unfamiliar, and equally complex improvisation:

> after we had formed
> then only the forms were formed
> and all the forms
> were formed after our forming . . . (57)

Egudu sees some similarities between this utterance and that in biblical language.[5] For example, he takes to the first person plural pronoun 'we,' and alludes to the collective 'us' of Genesis chapter one, to conclude that this voice is in another way expressing a philosophy, that it represents the 'Alpha and Omega.' Anozie believes this to be a deeper explanation of the question: what is the meaning of the symbol in the white chamber? (147) For him, those objects in the chamber had only been shaped after their maker was formed and, 'they are meant to express nothing but that form.' Conversely AnneMarie Heywood refers to the 'abnormality' of usage, lack of 'a coherent sentence,'[6] and takes up an Edmund Leach suggestion,[7] to conclude that there might be no intended meaning here: nonlogicality is in itself 'part of the code.'

Whatever its truth, this enigmatic riddle is bound up with creativity, and like an improvisator's innate power to continuously create, it appears to make a statement about the process of spontaneous artistic creativity. The figure at the archway is a symbol of this artistic creativity, its shape does not conform to given notions of form. But it is not meant to do so. In the same way that the response to this figure is prejudiced by preconceived notions of creative order (i.e. it is judged with notions of 'the cross' in mind), a fuller appreciation of Okigbo's work might depend on one's willingness to approach it in a 'new' way, 'without passing through that process of intellectual analysis.'[8]

When the solo voice is heard the final time in opus VI, it reassumes its primary purpose as chief explicator just before the process of "Distances" comes to an end. This is a lucid voice which invites the acolyte to engage in the final symbolic act, a signal perhaps as Gerald Moore suggests, that the initiate is prepared to receive her embrace[9]:

come into my cavern
shake the mildew from your hair;
Let your ear listen:
My mouth calls from a cavern . . . (59)

The background strains of inauspicious references and allusions, often to prophetic literature, are as embellishing to the texture of verse as any other motif which is sounded throughout "Distances."

'Dan to Beersheba,' 'the crucifix,' 'locusts,' 'abyss,' 'swords,' 'incense,' 'censer,' 'marble,' 'celestial,' and 'sanctuary' are some of the items from within "Distances I" to VI whose inclusion infuse an apocalyptic tinge. In "Distances II" death is foreboded when personified as 'lying in ambush' and 'paring her fingernails.' Images of gloom and blood hover over and taint every scene leading up to "Distances V," where the mood of the macabre is heightened by a most disturbing image of affection, betrayal and death in 'the scar of the kiss.' These images readily surface in the nebula of evening (and as in "Distances III"), this is a time frame which seems perennial. In fact a sense of timelessness exists throughout, from "Distances I" where a feeling of vacuity, abstraction and endless inner spaces is introduced by the Labyrinth symbol, to "Distances VI" where it reappears as 'the orangery of immense corridors' through which the acolyte has groped for what appears to be 'several centuries.'

Okigbo's is above all a music which plays on the senses. Its creation of fantasies through synesthaesia in 'water's laughter,' the 'air's marrow' and such images might border on magical realism.

The 'catatonic ping pong' in "Distances IV" and 'music woven into funerary rose' in "Distances V" are few of the literal allusions to music within this section, but they spell the dying of a practice left out at the end of "Limits," where the gods 'lie in state/without the long-drum.' If this is symbolic of the need for a resuscitation of the Igbo self, then "Distances" is an exercise in meeting this need by attempting to reconnect the initiate with his soul source, and the spirit of his ancestors through the use of 'the music of the long-drums.' The music of the long-drum becomes a symbol of traditional practices, of which total acknowledgement (if not acceptance) must be confessed by the artist as a prerequisite to achieving a total artistic outpouring. Quite significantly "Distances VI" concludes with the initiate's celebratory song. If Fraser's statement about Okigbo's tone of 'rejoicing' is not necessarily true of all of "Distances," it certainly holds true for this latter segment of "Distances VI," where the initiate celebrates a closer union with his soul through a medium lost within "Limits" but regained here. He sings:

> I have fed out of the drum
> I have drunk out of the cymbal
>
> I have entered your bridal
> chamber; and lo,
>
> I am the sole witness to my homecoming. (60)

NOTES

1. In his introduction to *Labyrinths*, Okigbo makes a fleeting reference to Lorca's influence. In his essay on "Fantasy or Dialectic" Anozie briefly refers to Okigbo's and Lorca's similarity as being based on the notion of possession, see *Labyrinths* (London: Heinemann, 1971). Also, Sunday Anozie's "Distances: Fantasy or Dialectic," *Critical Perspectives on Christopher Okigbo*, ed. Donatus Nwoga (Washington: Three Continents Press, 32).
2. Okigbo in his interview with Robert Serumaga, July 1965.
3. Leopold Senghor deals with this phenomenon in *La Parole Chez Claudel et Chez les Negro Africaines* (Dakar: Nouvelles Editiones Africaines, 1973), pp. 50-51.
4. Robert Fraser, *West African Poetry* (Cambridge: Cambridge University Press, 1986), p. 127.
5. Romanus Egubu, "Okigbo's Distances: A Retreat from Christ to Idoto," *Critical Perspectives*, p. 159.
6. Anne-Marie Heywood, "The Ritual and the Plot: The Critic and Okigbo's *Labyrinths*" *Critical Perspectives*, p. 214.
7. Edmund Leach, *Culture and Communication* (London: Cambridge University Press, 1976), pp. 70-74.
8. Okigbo in his interview with Serumaga.
9. Gerald Moore, "Vision and Fulfilment," *Critical Perspectives*, pp. 285-86.

J.P. Clark's *Song of a Goat:* A Study

S. SREERAMULU

The origins of African drama are not different from Greek drama or European drama in general. Aristotle in his *Poetics* traces the origin of Greek drama to the communal celebration of Dionysus which gave place to formal acting. The plays of Sophocles, Euripides and Aeschylus belong to the formal and written tradition of drama. African societies traditionally celebrated harvest and agricultural seasons with song and dance. The entire community participated in the performance. People wore masks, sported traditional "agbada" and sang and danced to the accompaniment of drums and horns. Besides the communal performance there was also the tradition of story-telling. Often the story-teller chose the story of a mythological character or a historical character whose life and adventure formed the basis of his narration. It is to be noted that the story-teller played the role of a central character and of other characters as well. Thus he was playing the twin roles of narrator and actor.

Unlike a modern play which is time bound and which is governed by classical rules of the unities of time, place and action, the African oral performance lasted for several nights and the audience sat through the performance. Not only the narrator lived the role he played but made the audience identify with the character he represented. Thus there was a close relationship between the actor and the audience.

Another important development in the history of African drama is that festival drama and ritual theatre which for a long time confined to their respective communities later evolved into travelling companies, Joel Adedegi who has worked on Yoruba theatre discusses the basis of the travelling companies and suggests that they had derived from "Alarinjo" theatre, travelling groups of entertainers, which grew out of the Yoruba court and cult performances after 16, 17, 18 centuries.

Hubert Ogunde's is the foremost among a very large number of travelling theatre companies. His theatre shows the influences of western dramatic modes combined with the Alarinjo theatre. The Egungun and Gelede, masquerades and the music traditions of the different kingdoms in Yoruba land exercised a great deal of influence. It is Ogunde who started the dialogue drama. Ogunde's theatre reflected the modes of the people of western Nigeria between 1946 to 1966. He changed the style, the form and the content of his work to suit the territory in which he performed. He concretized a number of political issues through characterization and story to Yoruba audiences. In all that he performed, there is Ogunde's personality. There are four phases in the development of Ogunde's theatre: (1) the phase of cultural nationalism from 1944-50 (2) consolidation of the company through independence from 1954-64 (3) post-independence party politics 1964 to 66 (4) The company since the civil war 1972 and later.

Though Ogunde's first plays were folk opera meant for the church, his plays *Strike and Hunger* performed in 1945 had political dimension. It presented the hopeless conditions of labour in colonial Nigeria and it inspired the general strike of 1945. His play *Tiger's Empire* also attacked colonialism. The company he started called the "African Music Research Party" indicated Ogunde's interest in Yoruba music which had been downgraded by the colonialists. He wanted his company to reawaken interest in Nigerian culture and support the movement for political and economic independence. He produced plays throughout west Africa between 1945-76 and made his roots in traditional festival drama quite clear.

J.P. Clark's work is not as large as Wole Soyinka's but it is nearer African life. He started writing poetry while he was an undergraduate at University College, Ibadan. Some of his early poems made liberal life of imagery from his childhood and they show the basic pattern of his early poetry: structure based upon occasion, imagery drawn from the river or from mythology, and heightened fear or dissatisfaction: within grief, chaos, insecurity, and irredeemable loss are the hallmarks of Clark's early poetry. Poems such as "Abiku Fulani Cattle," "Agbor Dancer" and "The Imprisonment Obalala" show Clark's enduring merit. He tried a wonderful variety of styles with success. His early poems were followed by the publication of the one act *Song of a Goat*. In his last years in the Ibadan University, Clark had seen the performances of plays by J.M. Synge and W.B. Yeats. He had also read the playwrights as a part of his course. Synge's interest in the tragic and comic aspects of Irish folk and Yeats's interest in Irish folklore influenced Clark that he was inspired to write *The Song of a Goat*.

The Song of a Goat reads like a Greek tragedy because as in the latter, man is pitted against forces beyond his control. It is unlike Shakespeare's tragedies in which the tragedy is caused partly because of the hero's inherent weakness. Othello's weakness is jealousy. Macbeth has an over-reaching ambition. King Lear is credulous and Hamlet suffers from inaction. So in a typical Shakespearean tragedy the hero himself invites the doom and destruction on himself. In a Greek tragedy, often the hero is a victim of a family curse or an heir to the sins of his parents. The hero, therefore, battles against unseen forces and fails.

The Song of a Goat is reminiscent of Greek tragedies. Zifa has become impotent after fathering a son. He can no longer produce children. This is the central issue and the entire play revolves round resolving this crisis. In the conflict that ensues, Zifa finds himself isolated and has to fight a host of opponents all of whom belong to his family. So ultimately it turns out to be not individual against society but the individual against his own family.

In the first movement there are two characters—Masseur, a man with extraordinary powers, including powers of healing, and Ebiere, Zifa's wife who has come to seek medical counsel from Masseur. After examining Ebiere, Masseur tells her that her "Womb is open and warm as room." (3) He allays her fears and assures her that there is nothing wrong with her. But he warns her against staying empty:

An empty house, my daughter, is a thing
Of danger. If men will not live in it
Bats or grass will, and that is enough
Signal for worse things to come in

Ebiere pleads that it is not her fault and she has always kept the doors open, "my house open by night and day," but her husband has kept away from her. She is ashamed of herself and even wishes to die if only to prevent people from taking her for a sterile woman. She admits that her husband has been avoiding her. Initially she thinks that her husband avoided her because of the problem she had in bringing forth her son. But later she realises that there is a deeper reason. After hearing her, Masseur corrects her and assures her that there is no shame in revealing this fact to her families. He goes even a little further to say "a good proposition/would be for your husband to make you over/To another in his family." (5) Ebiere is shocked to hear such an advice and rejects it:

That will be an act of death,
It is what dead forbid you speak of

To assuage her moral sense Masseur suggests a ritual which has the sanction of tradition and which will free her from immorality:

> So large a Cowrie may pass Blood of a goat through its nose
> A big gourd of palm wine and three heads of
> Kola-nut split before the dead of
> The land, and the deed is done.

But Ebiere is not prepared to accept the advice and so she leaves the place. Now Zifa comes in search of his wife and Masseur broaches the subject of impotence. Zifa says that he is helpless since there is no remedy for it. He might restore his former virility and beget children. But Masseur reminds him that it has been several seasons now and he has not regained his manliness. There is no birth cure for his wife "When the fault is not with her." However Zifa is hopeful and he cites the example of Ogun's wife who gave birth to children after seven years of waiting.

Masseur however makes a distinction between Ogun and Zifa. While Ogun never abandoned his wife, Zifa was guilty of it. Moreover Ogun's family has a curse and it had to be removed to have more children. Zifa too remembers Ogun's story and is eager to have a cure for himself. He says that he would offer the best sacrifice to cast off the curse. He narrates how he has been a loving husband and has consulted all experts on the land. He has been advised to adjust himself to his curse. He is sad that he is being punished for his father's sins. People who dared not oppose his father when he was alive accuse the son for honouring his father. While pitying Zifa, Masseur advises him to consider handing over his wife to another person. Zifa becomes angry at the suggestion and heaps curses on Masseur. But Masseur assures Zifa that it has the traditional sanction. Zifa refuses to reconcile to this idea and thinks that his death will solve the problem. But Zifa advises him to think coolly and act on his advice.

In the second movement, an important mystical character begins the action of the play just as Masseur, another mystical character, opened the first movement. The elderly, wise, experienced Masseur symbolizes tradition and is eager to guide his society. His being a physician is not literal but spiritual. He understands the malady affecting the family of Zifa and so offers a cure. Orukorere on the other hand is semi-mystical. She appears other-worldly in her behaviour but is also very realistic. As Zifa's aunt, she is concerned about the family, the impotence of her nephew.

As the second movement opens, Orukorere is shown crying for help. She has heard a cry of a goat. Both Zifa and his brother Tonye are annoyed at her cries. However Orukorere continues her cries and says that she continues to hear the cries of a goat. The neighbours who gather cannot understand her and they hear nothing but she insists that a goat is held by a leopard. When the neighbours begin to take Orukorere and the threat of the leopard seriously, Zifa attributes her behaviour to drinking. He is angry that the people have been helping her with free drinks but the neighbours reply that no one has given her drink. They even say that a drink is not available even for sacrifice. One goes to the extent of saying that she does not need a drink to behave this way. Orukorere stands by her vision and insists on the search for the leopard:

> I must find him the leopard
> That will devour my goat, I must
> Find him. Surely his footsteps will show
> Upon the mud? Surely, those claws bloodly
> From hunt of antelopes in the forest
> Will show in the sand? Or has the wind
> Swept them off before housewives come
> Upon them with brooms at break of day?
> Or sports him no spoors?

Orukorere has double vision as has been suggested by the Third Neighbour. She anticipates some threat to the family and her reference to the leopard again and again is a warning to the family. Soon after to everybody's surprise she passes on and it looks very strange to every one. The neighbours want Zifa to act at once but Zifa prays to the spirits of his village to advise as to what he should do. The neighbours begin to leave after advising Zifa to take care of her. Now she is foaming in the mouth and shivering. They all comment that there is a curse on the family and it is this curse which has made the "sweetest maid" become queer woman. Many young men had offered to marry her but she refused to marry any. It is her father's curse which has made her life like that. Not only had she refused to marry human beings she refused also "the people of the sea." As a punishment the people of the sea have put a spell on her. In a long dialogue involving so many neighbours it may be gathered that Oruko has extraordinary powers of prophecy.

From Orukorere, the focus shifts to Ebiere. The neighbours have noted how queer she has become and how she looks very stiff and acquired clary colour. All these suggest that Ebiere is not the same woman that she was. All those who have been commenting get away like goats before ants on seeing Ebiere. She is also told about Orukorere's crying by her son, Dode. She is not surprised because she has been such a thing before. She is all sympathy for her. She says:

> The woman is almost a child once more
> Why, yes. Any one can see that from how she behaves
> And for that alone I get rather fond of her (20)

Zifa also agrees with his wife and says so to his brother.

While the three discuss Orukorere, Dode brings up the news that she is up and sinking. Now Orukorere comes out of her trance and tells them that she has missed the leopard. She adds that she is not a proper leopard but might be a snake. As she sets out of the house, she asks for money but is refused.

In the third movement, there is a domestic scene with Ebiere scolding Dode for playfulness. She complains that he does not know how to bathe but knows how to eat all through the day. She is so annoyed with his behaviour that she knocks him on the head. Tonye who has been watching the mother and the son chides Ebiere for her rudeness. He even boasts that children in his family are well taken care of. At this, Ebiere makes a hissing sound and Tonye taunts her that she is like a snake and her hissing suggests spite and sinister notice. What he cannot understand is that such a thing should come from a housewife and he is innocent of her meaning. At this Ebiere expresses her helplessness in the family. But the lack of sympathy is common to everyone in the family. Tonye does not understand the cause of her misery. Ebiere now comes out openly and tells him how she has not been able to bring forth children after the only child. She says:

> Thus the elders pray: only one seed
> The elephant brings forth at a time until
> The house is full, yes, until the house be
> Full even if this takes ten falls of the flood

The analogy with the elephant is indicative of her disappointment with the only child. Tonye advises Ebiere to give up all thoughts of more children and take care of her child and husband properly. He finds fault with her for neglecting them and not cooking regularly. Stung by criticism of her irregular ways, she counters him:

> Of course, it is the woman who is in the wrong
> Always—I have suffered neglect and
> Gathered mould like a thing of sacrifice
> Left out in sun and rain at the cross-roads
> You talk to me of my short temper; what
> Short temper have I when it is pulled and
> Tugged at daily like a hook line?

No longer content with indirect suggestions, Ebiere now provokes Tonye to take up the duties of his brother. She demands that he must prove his strength and manliness. Initially he resists Ebiere's provocation but ultimately yields to her. Orukorere hears about it from Dode and closes the door for them. Although she has not prevented Ebiere and Tonye from the sexual act, she realises that it is a sign of woman's great betrayal of her rage. Pleading her helplessness to separate Tonye and Ebiere and feeling pity for Zifa, she remembers how there was a forewarning of all this earlier:

> I said there was
> A serpent in the house but nobody as usual
> Will take me seriously. Yet the hiss of the creature
> Was up among the caves, down under the
> Stool. Last night I cried it had coiled itself
> into a pad to pillow my head but the house
> Was full of snoring sound and as usual
> Everybody snorted.

In the climactic final movement, Zifa discovers the truth. The adulterous relationship between his brother Tonye and his wife incenses him. What is more hurting than his brother's conduct is his wife's concern for his brother. He cannot understand the change that has come over. She had always been critical of Tonye but

> Now she stands
> Guard over him in my bed against him

Zifa spares to kill both of them. Orukorere, unaware of Zifa's anger, reminds everyone to get ready for the market. She thinks that Zifa got up early to make offerings of sacrifice to those who guard the house. Zifa refers to his misfortunes "these many years" but his aunt advises him to be patient. Now Zifa comes out with cause for his anger which lies in the infidelity of his wife. He demands his aunt to tell him whatever had happened between his brother and his wife. Orukorere explains how she has tried her best to prevent the adultery. She instills courage in him and sooths him saying that only a goat cries when it is caught by a leopard. She tells him that he is not a goat and the strong do not weep.

After a very intimate scene between Zifa and his aunt in which both of them discuss the crisis in the family, there is a tense situation. The brothers Zifa and Tonye confront each other. While Tonye thinks that his brother is unaware of the adultery, Zifa is angry with his brother. Tonye insists on Ebiere going to the market to barter the fish for other provisions needed in the house but Zifa rejects it. The aunt pleads for patience and asks them not to follow.

From the conversation between Zifa and his aunt, it may be gathered that there is going to be a sacrifice. The house needs cleaning. When Zifa leaves for a while on a visit to the shrine Orukorere is unhappy at the turn of events. She says that several transgressions have been committed in the house. She involves her dead brother to tell him how fortunate he is in the other world. If he were alive he would find his sons "like bad fish eating one and another." Meanwhile, there is the goat crying and she must leave to find a live chicken to carry out the ritual.

It is ironical that while everyone in the family knows about their guilt, Ebiere and Tonye delude themselves in the belief that no one knows about their affair. Ebiere even suggests to Tonye that they could run away and "set up house in another week." Tonye will catch fish and they will have their child. Tonye warns against such a move since Zifa does not want Ebiere to go to market. Then Ebiere tells him that Zifa will leave on his ship and before he returns they might fly. Now Zifa returns and is in querulous mood. He tells his aunt that he will now make sacrifice to the gods. He has long ignored the advice to that effect. But Orukorere reminds him that he is not cleansed yet. It is harmful and rash to go against the custom. But Zifa is in a hurry. He asks his brother and his wife to hold the goat by the feet and horns. Once the sacrifice is performed Zifa is confident that the corruption is removed. Zifa asks his brother Tonye to put the goat's head with all its horns into the pot. Ebiere and Tonye are surprised by Zifa's command because they know that it is difficult to push the goat's head into the pot. While Tonye is at it, Ebiere fails. Orukorere asks Tonye to run away lest he should be killed by Zifa. Tonye begins to flee. He looks himself up in a room. Zifa warns him that he will break open the door and kill him. Orukorere now calls out the people. People gather and they understand what has happened. Towards the end of the play, we find that Tonye has hanged himself and Ebiere never recovers but dies. Zifa himself walks into the sea.

The Song of a Goat is firmly rooted in the Nigerian soil. The characters, situations, problems are all authentic. The Ijaw beliefs in curses, spirits and ritual offerings form the texture of the play. Clark builds the plot to its climax by a series of movements, each movement ending with arousing expectation of future events. The play has a sense of doom as every character is powerless and caught in a web which he cannot break. The dramatic quality gains its strength from the poetry of play. Like the tragic hero in a Greek play, the central character Zifa is a plaything for gods. For the Nigerians, the play reflects the cardinal value of family—for the men to bring about strong breed and for women to be faithful to their men.

Drama and the Yoruba Worldview: Soyinka's Ritual Metaphysics and the Cultural Cross-Currents in Yoruba Theatre History

DEREK WRIGHT

At the outset of his first book of critical essays, *Myth, Literature and the African World*, Wole Soyinka poses "the perennial question of whether ritual can be called drama, at what moment a religious or mythic celebration can be considered transformed into drama."[1] Of course, even allowing for the complex interweavings of religious and theatrical forms in the Yoruba world, a rite is not instant drama, nor ritual movement ballet, and in his festival field-work Soyinka has been at pains to point this out, observing that initiation rituals and traditional dances contain rudimentary performance elements but no finished artistic form.[2] In the two essays "Ritual Archetypes" and "Drama and the African Worldview" which make up the first half of *Myth, Literature and the African World*, however, Soyinka's pervasive tendency is to collapse conventional division between magical drama and dramatic art, religion and theatre, cult and culture. Furthermore, in his earlier essay "The Fourth Stage," attached to the book as an Appendix, his visionary conception of the actor as ritual celebrant creates some uncertainty as to whether the terms are merely analogical or whether a more literal link between cultic rites (the drama of the gods) and theatre (the human drama) is being claimed; whether ritual is being likened to drama or *is* that thing; and whether, in the last analysis, a rite is about reality, like a play, or is its own reality. In this short article I propose to examine briefly the relationship of Soyinka's ritual metaphysics to his writing on cultural and theatrical history, and to see what light is shed upon this by the complex historical interactions and continuities between Yoruba dramatic forms.

No doubt with a cautious eye on the carnival elements, the mock-battles and wanton revelry, of some festivals (e.g. the Ogun one), Soyinka issues the somewhat grudging proviso at the beginning of his book that "casual secular entertainments may also involve the gods" who are "quite amenable to fustian." (5) He does not, however, in this instance attempt to derive Yoruba drama historically from the pseudo-illusionist modes and primitive satiric of the secular masquerade. Words like "derive" and "originate" are, in any case, barren particularizations in the creative context of Soyinka's infinitely optional, visionary metaphysics. It would be more accurate to say that in his essay "The Fourth Stage," he "extracts" or "extrudes" a concept of tragic drama—more a distillation of essences than a derivation of particulars—from the consecrated component or cultic "Mysteries" of the festival rites dedicated to the god Ogun. His tendency is to focus exclusively, and somewhat ahistorically, upon one part of the ritual model—the sacral, cultic phase—but in such a way as to subsume all other elements into it, so that it comes to stand for the whole ritual experience and to serve as the fountainsprings of Yoruba drama.

From the outset of his essay "Drama and the African Worldview" Soyinka affects a strong antihistorical bias. The African's understanding of "irreducible truths" and "fundamental, unchanging relationships between himself and society and within the larger context of the observable universe" are given preference over Western "period dialectics," as if history were not a dimension of theatre development as of everything else. (38) It appears that we are being invited into a realm of timeless essences where the transfer from ritual to drama has never and has always taken place; where ritual, insofar as it has always contained the inherent possibility of drama within itself, is eternally drama and drama ritual. But the apparently glib metaphysics really mask deeper historical perceptions. Soyinka's argument is that the question of the dividing line between these two properties is only a problem for cultures that have divorced drama from its ritual roots and need to reestablish points of demarcation in order, by diverse artificial methods, to recover them (Soyinka instances Genet's plays and Peter Brook's *Orghast*). The implication is that this is not a problem and can be no more than an academic issue for cultures in which those roots are still visibly present. There is historical substance in this. In the pluralistic setting of contemporary Yoruba drama, for example (as, indeed, in Nigeria and on the African continent at large,) the oldest autocthonous, hieratic forms of ritual theatre still coexist, as in a cultural time warp, with the sophisticated dramaturgy of the modern literary theatre. Theoretically, it is still possible for a modern audience at one of Duro Ladipo's dynastic Yoruba plays or at an English language play like Soyinka's own *A Dance of the Forests* to measure the various stylized and hybridized borrowings from ancient legends, folk motifs and ritual practices against their "pure" originals, still extant in their festival forms. Preoccupied as he is with these threads of timelessness that are woven into the fabric of history, Soyinka is not concerned in this context to investigate the physical transposition of ritual within the African world: for example, the dynamics of displacement from its primordial habitat in sacred grove, shrine or point of historical origin, first to festival contexts and from thence to the fenced arena of the modern theatre. Neither is he much interested in the practical question of how, or if, the intimate communal catharsis of the ritual survives its restaging in the alienatory settings of auditorium and amphitheatre. For answers to such questions, we have to go to dramaturgical critics like Annemarie Heywood, who argues that all mask idioms become non-naturalistic and anti-empathetic when removed to stage settings and to production modes that are not designed to elicit catharsis (she advises, accordingly, that Soyinka's own plays be played in the anti-illusionist Brechtian manner, with operatic acting styles and emblematic movement).[3]

Yet if the main thrust of Soyinka's metaphysical refinements from Ogun festivals go quite against the grain of conventional Yoruba theatre history as written by academic historians, it should be added that they also run counter to what has been written on the subject, elsewhere and in a different persona, by Soyinka himself. In his more historical-minded essay, "Theatre in African Traditional Cultures: Survival Patterns," Soyinka opts to follow the Yoruba theatre historian Joel Adedeji in tracing Yoruba drama to a form of Masque Theatre which allegedly emerged not from the sacral rites but from the secular masquerade of egungun funeral obsequies at the Oyo royal court in the early seventeenth century; by the mid-nineteenth century, it is claimed, the splinter movement had ramified into travelling troupes of performing masqueraders such as the *Alarinjo* and *Agbegijo*, some of which are still active, though much in decline, at the present day. (191)[4] According to this later essay, this "pagan" masquerade dramaturgy was the main stronghold of cultural resistance to the rival religious repressions of Arab and European colonialism and "has continued until today to vitalize contemporary theatrical forms both in the tradition of 'folk opera' and in the works of those playwrights and directors commonly regarded as 'Westernized'." (190) To the identical vexed question of "when a performed event became theatre as ritualism." Soyinka here answers that dating the origin of African drama, locating it in specific event and place, has been made impossible by historical imponderables such as the vagaries of the colonial dispersal of the egungun masquerades. (191, 194) The approach this time is a solidly historical one, even if the evidence is disputed and provides no reliable answers. Soyinka is, respectively, metaphysician and cultural historian in these essays, writing in the dual critical modes of the "mystical-metaphysical" and the "social-historical," and it is not unusual for metaphysics to fly in the face of history in the search for more profound poetic and philosophical truths not available to its empirical method. Moreover, Soyinka is a notoriously protean, many-sided figure, rich in contradiction, and it is never safe to assume that ideas propounded in one context will necessarily be consistent with material relating to the same ideas in a different one.

It is of course arguable that the close derivation of tragic drama from religious ritual which Soyinka, like J.P. Clark, takes as axiomatic is itself a Western notion, based on Aristotle's and Nietzsche's readings (respectively, technical and visionary, dramaturgical and Dionysiac) of the Greek dithyramb.[5] But this does not mean that a similar emergence, proceeding from different ritual premises and under different cultural conditions, did not take place in Africa. Soyinka, whether his mode of argument be metaphysical or historical, is no Western evolutionist in his dramatic thinking. It is understood that "ritual" (as "African") is not to be seen as existing in negative and primitive conjunction with the "developed" form of "drama" (as "European"), but is in its essence inseparable from and so interchangeable with it. At a pragmatic level, Soyinka is not only mindful of his own debts to traditional forms and symbolism. He has seriously doubted, in his cultural polemic, whether it is correct to see the non-dialogic masquerade dramaturgy of festivals, after the Western fashion, as the primitive ingredients or raw material of modern drama; that is, as an embryonic "predrama," a historical halfway house between religion and theatre, lacking the full dramatic pedigree that would admit of a fruitful continuity with sophisticated literary forms. Taking a whimsical look for a moment down the "wrong" end of the historical telescope in his essay on traditional African theatre, Soyinka evaluates the festival's prodigal resources and high levels of organization and community involvement, its artistic stylization of events to a point far beyond ritual necessity, and its raising of everyday life to a more intense and symbolically expressive level of reality; and then ponders expansion. from its supposed origins. (194-95)

The conventional evolutionist and culturally denigrating Western view of drama was, however, the one that prevailed in the early criticism of post-Independence Nigerian theatre. Western anthropologists and literary critics writing of African drama in the early 1960s, though sometimes making an exception of West Africa, tended to relegate non-sequential, non-dialogic festival dramaturgy to the category of "pre-drama" or "quasi-drama." By this was understood something not quite removed from its ritual roots but not fully worked through into full-blooded performance and therefore yet to be awarded the full dramatic status that would licence its incorporation into literary drama like Soyinka's.[6] Though not entirely beyond the domain of drama, festival theatricals were in this view only potentially dramatic ("pre" was used in the sense of "preschool" rather than "prehistoric"). The bequest from this kind of dramaturgy to more sequential and representational Europeanized forms was acknowledged, but this bequest was supposed to consist chiefly in selected performance skills rather than in any shaping vision or structure design. During the same period, some other Western critics out in the field were only too ready to concede full status to traditional dramaturgy, but expressed some regret that the dramatists themselves had not done so, with the result that traditional material had percolated too slowly into the modern theatre.[7] Their opinions received an impetus from a prevailing notion among Nigerian critics of the period that there had developed in the new nation a "two cultures" situation, as a result of which the purity of popular art forms in the indigenous culture had been protected by their isolation from, and independence of, the more elite forms cultivated by the borrowed Western culture.[8] According to this view, both "folk opera" in Yoruba and literary drama in English were foreign forms because neither had developed in direct response to native products, and there was a tendency to assume that they and indigenous drama were discontinuous and mutually exclusive.

The truth in fact was more complex. Indeed, the modern cultural and theatrical situation in Nigeria has proved bewilderingly complex and it has never been possible to assume total discontinuity between traditional ritual dramaturgy and modern literary theatre, or between popular indigenous and elite Western forms. Here the taxonomist runs into problems because myth and folklore, festival masquerade and oral narrative, folk theatre and drama in English all have common points of contact in the circular, holistic maze of Yoruba religious art and all incorporate "traditional" elements in one way or another. Myths are made drama in their enactment by ritual, and are themselves accumulations of folklore. This folklore in turn supplies from its reservoir of proverbial oral wisdoms the incantatory chants and praise songs of festivals—the *oriki, ewi, ijala*, and even some sacred *odu* of Ifa oracle—and these chants and songs then find their way back into folk drama.[9] There are no theatrical thorough-breds along this spectrum, only hybrids and half-castes, and a sometimes bewildering degree of cross fertilization. Even if the critic's survey starts from the "purist" position that festival mask drama draws its impetus from ritual and folk theatre, from myth and folk narrative, and modern anglophone drama from the Western theatre, it is not long before the lines begin to get crossed and the genres clouded. All of these forms have been, literally or metaphorically, travelling theatres, protean in their capacity to assimilate influences both old and new on their national and international itineraries. The folk theatre of Hubert Ogunde, Kola Ogunmola, and Duro Ladipo had, it is true, originally evolved not from any native product but out of secularized mission school and church drama, and its immediate impetus came from the narrative thrust of folklore, not the ritual one of festival.[10] However, it borrowed retrospectively from the dramaturgical traditions of the masquerade. Ogunde, the father of the "folk opera" (who performed his play *The Garden of Eden* in Abeokuta Town Hall in Soyinka's tenth year), had been an *Alarinjo* masquerader in his youth, and his Concert Party theatre was something of a historical blind alley until it was invigorated by injections of the raw and robust burlesque, the grotesquely stylized movements, and the acrobatic dance for which the *Alarinjo* had become famous. In his later essay on traditional African theatre, Soyinka demurred that some of Ogunde's masquerade additions of the early sixties were "gratuitous insertions." (202) But in a 1975 discussion he expressed the unorthodox view, once more against the grain of Yoruba theatre scholarship, that folk theatre did not merely take festival dramaturgy under its wing but actually developed out of it, and proceeded to describe his own theatre as an attempt to combine this festival/folk hybrid with the more technically advanced drama.[11] Even in his earliest interview, in 1962, Soyinka viewed as an inevitable step the incorporation of traditional masquerade idioms—ritual, dance, and mime—into the pattern of modern theatre.[12] The more culturally pure mythological folk theatre of Ladipo, with which Soyinka's own theatre company worked closely in the 1960s, improvised plays around ritual chants and songs, often with an eye to original festival forms. Ladipo's Oba Koso utilized incantation and trance in much the same way as Soyinka's *Death and the King's Horseman*, which is in fact a reworking of historical material dealt with in Ladipo's earlier *Oba Waja*. Kola Ogunmola's popular moral satires had obvious common ground with the satiric masquerade in their combination of *presentational* and *representational* modes, creating entertaining stage presences as ends in themselves as well as fully realized characters. But there was also, in the opposite direction, a clear line of development from these popular entertainment medlies to Soyinka's revue sketches, *Opera Wonyosi*, and the *Jero* plays, as is evident in a number of features: for example, the anti-illusionist acting styles, moving actors back and forth between character and choric roles and having them directly address the audience (folk theatre is inherently Brechtian); and the episodic structures, with their serial climaxes and loose assemblage of vignettes.

Given the broad, interpenetrative continuity of theatrical development in Yorubaland, it is not surprising to find Soyinka, in his essay on traditional African theatre, writing of the breakaway-emergence of Ogunde's Concert Party from Christian worship in the 1940s as being part of the same continuing process as, and therefore identical with, the parallel evolution of the *Agbegijo* mask theatre from Oyo royal funeral rites three centuries earlier. (198) Neither is it all odd to discover Soyinka, never an armchair dramatist, working in the same combined capacity of writer-actor-manager-director as the giants of the folk theatre and adopting some of their production techniques. The hit-and-run style of Soyinka's 1970s guerilla theatre—the limited cautious publicity and risk-taking polemics, the lightning presentation of what are effectively corporate creations, minimally scripted and rehearsed and constantly modified in performance—are all in the best Ogunde and *Alarinjo* travelling traditions. But the formative influences that turn on the popular/modern and folk/literary axes are not all one way. Episodes such as the egungun sequences in *The Road* demonstrated the capacity of the illusion-conjuring technology of Western theatre to bring out ritual dramaturgy's expressive drama in emotional power of a frightening intensity. Accordingly, there has been ample feedback from the more technically-endowed university theatres into the stage technology of the travelling folk theatres (notably in the multimedia theatre of Moses Olaiya), and the feedback from scripted drama has even extended to festival ritual: it is discernible, for example, in the appearance of more complex dialogic elements in the masquerades of relatively new festivals.[13]

As a result of this unceasing hybridization and circular influence, it is extremely difficult to say exactly what came when in Yoruba drama and what was derived from what. Extant dramatic modes and styles, whatever their origin or age, are not static, finished products. In the hands of highly eclectic, malleable hosts like the travelling theatre companies, they are constantly being re-formed and regrouped into new syntheses, and it has consequently become unrealistic to talk in terms of narrowly "ritual" or "folk," or even "Afrocentric" and "Eurocentric" models. These mutually interactive modes are most accurately conceived as simultaneously existing, and concurrently advancing and adapting. In *Myth, Literature and the African World*, Soyinka humorously caricatures the compartmentalized habits of Western evolutionist thinking about drama as a steam engine, lurching forward in "a series of intellectual spasms" as it shunts very short distance between historical stations to pick up successive theatrical cargoes of ritual, allegory, naturalism, surrealism, and absurdism. (37-38) It would be a bold critic who would risk riding the evolution engine through the history of African drama in an endeavour to trace, for example, a direct line of descent from pure ritual at one end of the scale to literary drama at the other. Even the most crooked course—from breakaway egungun groups as court obsequies through travelling masquerade troupes and folk theatre—would record few of the complex couplings, reversals, sideways shunts, detours and derailments along the way. The journey metaphor is itself suspect as it cannot do justice to the complex lateral interweavings of religious and theatre history, and of hermetic and popular forms, or to the process of random selection which exploits the theatrical potential of some ritual practices and not others. It is to Soyinka's credit that even in his blandest metaphysical moments he never entirely loses sight of Yoruba theatre's tortuous travel.

NOTES

1. Wole Soyinka, *Myth, Literature and the African World* (Cambridge: Cambridge University Press, 1976), p. 6.
2. Wole Soyinka, "Theatre in Traditional African Cultures," in his *Art, Dialogue and Outrage*: *Essays on Literature and Culture* (Ibadan: New Horn Press, 1988), p. 193 and "Five Minutes of Our Dances in a Theatre Will Chloroform You," *Daily Times* (Lagos), 7 July 1962.
3. Annemarie Heywood. "The Fox's Dance: The Staging of Soyinka's Plays," *Critical Perspectives on Wole Soyinka*, ed. James Gibbs (Washington, D.C.: Three Continents Press, 1980), pp. 130-38.
4. Joel Adedeji, "Trends in the Content and Form of the Opening Glee in

Yoruba Drama," *Critical Perspectives on Nigerian Literatures*, ed. Bernth Lindfors (Washington, D.C: Three Continents Press, 1975), pp. 41-42; "*Alarinjo*: The Traditional Yoruba Travelling Theatre," *Theatre in Africa*, ed. Oyin Ogunba and Abiola Irele (Ibadan: Ibadan University Press, 1978), p. 27. A more detailed explication of Adedeji's hypothesis about the origins and development of the *Alarinjo* is provided in his unpublished Ph.D. thesis, "The *Alarinjo* Theatre: The Study of a Yoruba Theatrical Art from its Earliest Beginnings to the Present Times," University of Ibadan, 1969. Adedeji's theory about the funereal origins of masquerade dramaturgy and *Alarinjo* theatre in Oyo egungun rites has been strongly contested by Oyekan Owomoyela in his article "Creative Historiography and Critical Determinism in Nigerian Theatre," *Research in African Literature*, 17, 2 (1986), pp. 249-50.

5. Aristotle, "On the Art of Poetry," *Classical Literary Criticism*, trans. T.S. Dorsch (Harmondsworth: Penguin, 1965), pp. 32-33, 36-37; Friedrich Nietzsche, *The Birth of Tragedy* (1872), trans. Francis Golffing (New York: Doubleday Anchor, 1956), pp. 27-28.
6. John Ferguson, "Nigerian Drama in English," *Modern Drama*, 11 (May 1968), p. 10; Ruth Finnegan, *Oral Literature in Africa* (Oxford: Clarendon Press, 1970), p. 500.
7. Martin Banham, "A Piece That We May Fairly Call Our Own," *Ibadan*, 12 (June 1961), p. 18; "Notes on Nigerian Theatre: 1966," *BAALE* (Freetown) 4 (March 1966), pp. 33-34; Michael Crowder, "Tradition and Change in Nigerian Literature," *Tri-Quarterly*, 5 (1966), p. 117, 124-25; Molly Mahood, "Drama in Newborn States," *Presence Africaine*, 60 (1966), p. 33.
8. Oyin Ogunba, "Traditional African Festival Drama," in Ogunba and Irele, ed., *Theatre in Africa* (Ibadan: Ibadan University Press, 1978), pp. 4-5.
9. For examples of the complex circular interactions between folk and festival forms, see the following: Oyin Ogunda, "Theatre in Nigeria," *Presence Africaine*, 58 (1966), pp. 70-73; Ola Rotimi, "Traditional Nigerian Drama," *Introduction to Nigerian Literature*, ed. Bruce King (London: Evans, 1971), pp. 36-49; Joel Adedeji, "Oral Tradition and the Contemporary Theatre in Nigeria," *Research in Africian Literatures* 2, 2 (1971), pp. 136-37, 143-47; Oyekan Owomoyela, "Folklore and Yoruba Theatre," *Critical Perspectives on Nigerian Literatures*, ed. Bernth Lindfors, p. 33; Biodun Jeyifo, *The Yoruba Popular Travelling Theatre of Nigeria* (Lagos: Nigeria Magazine, 1984), pp. 15-22, 39-41, 98-105, 128-29.
10. Owomoyela, "Folklore and Yoruba Theatre," pp. 33-39.
11. Wole Soyinka, "Class Discussion," *In Person: Achebe, Awoonor and Soyinka at the University of Washington*, ed. Karen Morell (Seattle: Institute of Comparative and Foreign Area Studies), p.100.
12. "Wole Soyinka," *African Writers Talking*, ed. Dennis Duerden and Cosmo Pieterse (London: Heinemann, 1972), p. 170.
13. See, for example, Austin Asagba's account of the *Ame* Olokun Festival at

Sapele in "Roots of African Drama: Critical Approaches and Elements of Continuity," *Kunapipi*, 8, 3 (1986), pp. 88-89. For other instances of the feedback from modern literary theatre into folk and festival drama, and of the interplay between mask drama and folk theatre, see the following: Adedeji, "Oral Tradition and Contemporary Theatre in Nigeria," pp. 135-36; "Trends in the Content and Form of the Opening Glee in Yoruba Drama," pp. 52-55; "*Alarinjo*: The Traditional Yoruba Travelling Theatre," pp. 49-50; and Jeyifo, *The Yoruba Popular Travelling Theatre of Nigeria*, pp. 15-22, 39-41, 98-100, 128-29.

Black But Beautiful: Wole Soyinka

K. VENKATA REDDY

Among the recipients of Nobel Prize for 1986, perhaps none evoked a greater excitement and joy among the public than Wole Soyinka, a West African creative writer, who 'writes like an angel.' The happy news is all the more welcoming in the present context of the abominable apartheid which is rocking the Western world. However, the most covetous award of the Nobel Prize for Soyinka is not altogether surprising for those who knew that he had already won the John Campbell Award for his distinction as a novelist and the British Arts Council John Whiting Award for his distinction as a playwright.

Wole Soyinka is a poet, playwright, novelist, essayist, critic, editor and translator, all rolled into one. He is undoubtedly the greatest of contemporary African playwrights. He has been rightly hailed as 'one of the finest poetic playwrights who have ever written in English.' Soyinka has to his credit fifteen plays in which he has made extensive use of Yoruba mythology. His plays helped to develop a Nigerian theatre in which he presents the imposition of European civilization on Africa as a threat to the African villager's individuality.

Although Soyinka has been actively involved in the theatre, he has held several teaching posts and published two novels, two volumes of poetry, besides the notes of his prison experience. As Srinivasa Iyengar has rightly pointed out, "an 'existentialist' on his own, Soyinka can fuse poetry and memory and prophecy, highlighting the plight of modern man face-to-face with the glamour and glory and blight of the technological age."

Born in Abeokuta in 1934, Soyinka was educated in Ibadan and Leeds. On his return to Nigeria, after nearly six years in Europe, Soyinka was appointed to a number of University posts. He studied indigenous drama at the University College and resolved that he would revive. in a modern context, the native dramatic forms. As a University teacher. he was able to produce his own plays on stage, sometimes acting in them himself. He also worked for Nigerian radio and television and formed an acting company in Lagos called *The 1960 Masks*. Soyinka was arrested by the Federal Government in 1967, for alleged pro-Biafran activity. The result of his experiences in solitary confinement at Kadura prison is recorded with great bitterness in *The Man Died*. After his release from jail in 1969, Soyinka became Director of the School of Drama in the University of Ife. But, creative writing has been his passion as well as his vocation.

Soyinka started his dramatic career as a comic writer. His early plays, *The Swamp Dwellers* and *The Lion and the Jewel* deal with traditional village life experimenting with mime and dance elements as an integral part of the comedy. Particularly, *The Lion and the Jewel* is a rollicking comic satire of the clash between the self-indulgent, crafty but shrewd tribal chieftainship and the superficially Westernized at the primary school-master level.

Soyinka's plays had subsequently become more technically daring. *A Dance of the Forests*, his highly ambiguous celebration of Nigerian independence in 1960, dramatises a confrontation between the living and the dead, between history and reality. The play is about a village community's request to the gods to allow two of the dead ancestors of the clan to return to life to take part in a great communal feasting. Ironically enough the two chosen by the gods are a captain and his wife who, in their own lives centuries ago, were associated with violence. As it turns out, the guests of honour from the dead have come not to celebrate with the living but to accuse them of the crimes they commit in their daily lives. Thus, the mortal world and the divine are brought into conjunction in a half-satirical, half-fantastic blend of traditional Yoruba imagery, dance motifs and masque. Underneath it all runs Soyinka's caustic commentary on the violence and corruption of the very society whose incipient nationhood the play was commissioned to celebrate.

The ironical strain in the early Soyinka develops into the full, punishing satire in *Kongi's Harvest* (1967), a play about the power struggle between a modern dictatorial political leader and a traditional, semi-priest of a State, reminding us at times of T.S. Eliot's *Murder in the Cathedral*.

Now, to turn to Soyinka's 'magnum opus,' *The Road* is to move from the intensely comic and the satiric to the purely tragic and symbolic. Like Tagore's *The Post-Office*, Soyinka's *The Road* is a powerful symbolic piece, insinuating the subtle clash and sinister affiliations between primitive belief and African Christianity. With its distinct echoes of the Theatre of the Absurd, the play seeks to expose a world of a phantasmagoria of masked dance and muffled action, involving the clash of obscure powers and personalities.

The setting is a transport depot in a Nigerian town. In a garage where the salvaged parts of crashed cars are sold, the owner named Professor, an unorthodox Christian, is engaged in trying to understand the meaning of death. He is presented as a piece of motley, half-genuine and half-bogus, a fantastic mix of businessman, charlatan and prophet. In his role as prophet, Professor begins the maddening enactment of the Resurrection. He seeks the WORD, and is half-afraid it might turn out to be Death followed by the Resurrection. He is driven at last to use the pagan God, Ogun, to enact the Christian drama of Resurrection which explodes into melodrama. All the same, Professor somehow manages, in his own blundering and exasperated way, to convey the eternal cyclic truth of birth and change and death and renewal. The play is strewn with symbols. The road is a passage from somewhere to somewhere, and life too is a passage from somewhere to somewhere. The road is uncannily deceptive, and mankind can be deceptive too. This road's seductive bends and coils can be an invitation to destruction just as life's baits and temptations could be.

Soyinka's most significant dramatic work in recent years is *Madmen and Specialists* (1971) which is the measure of his success as an analyst of his society's ills. Soyinka's criticism of his society is at its most ferocious here. The play is primarily concerned with the physical, the mental and moral destruction of modern civil war. It evokes the terrible hurt that armed struggle between man and man causes to the human psyche, destroying it almost beyond recognition. It unfolds the clashing of rival motivations and the tangles of individuals' destinies, all racing towards the ignition of the final tragedy. The supreme merit of the play lies in the fact that it can still be read as a play articulating a grave warning to global mankind about the holocaust that will overwhelm civilization when the political power game risks our dear earth's future.

Thus, all Soyinka's plays evidence a social conscience. They deal with the problems that beset Nigerian society, particularly with the problems that have arisen, as traditional communities have been gradually transformed by developments in post-independent Nigeria. Nevertheless, their dramatic power to disturb and move the audience reaches beyond the specific problems of present-day Nigeria and touches on larger questions relating to the conduct of society and to the conscience of the individual and of the community.

As a novelist Soyinka has been the subject of some controversy. His novel, *The Interpreters*, is a multi-pronged satire against the sickness of Nigerian urban society. It is concerned with a group of young Nigerian intellectuals capturing their idealism, and their anticipation of the development of the new Africa. Soyinka's second novel, *Season of Anomy,* corresponds to his play, *Madmen and Specialists,* in its attempts to make sense of the recent devastation of war. It is an expression of the affirmative, humane response to chaos and blind social forces.

Idanre and Other Poems (1967) and *A Shuttle in the Crypt* (1972) are two of Soyinka's collections of verse, written over several years. Soyinka's poetry has a strong rhythmic and sensuous quality and derives many of its themes from Nigerian folklore. The tone of the second collection is even bleaker than the first, distilling not just the horrors and pity of war but the sterility of modern politics. *Idanre* is an extremely complex poem about knowledge and belief. Based partly on the experience of a night Soyinka spent among the Idanre hills in Nigeria and associated with the God, Ogun, the long poem seeks to resolve the paradox of harvest and fruitlessness amidst the violence and destruction of war.

Soyinka has always tried to express a broad humanity in his work which will not be narrowly nationalistic. Many of his cultural tenets are set out in an illuminating critical book, *Myth, Literature and the African World.* No doubt, Soyinka admits a recognizable distinction between African and European aesthetics, but he believes that they should not operate in isolation from each other.

Although by no means a spokesman for Negritude, Soyinka symbolizes Africa in both its outer form and its deeper soul and sensibility. In his plays, as also in Chinua Achebe's novels, we are led to see how the imposition of the civilization of the West has proved ruinous to Africa's long-tested way of life. And, what one of Soyinka's own characters says of black people: "I like black people, I really do. Black people are exciting, their colour has such vitality . . . something really beautiful, distinctive." We may as well say of Soyinka himself: 'we like Soyinka, we really do. He is exciting and has such vitality . . . something reallly beautiful, distinctive.' Soyinka is black but beautiful as a writer. What does his colour matter as long as he 'writes like an angel' and about 'African Heaven.' Let us sing with Frank Parkes, yet another exciting African writer:

> Give me black souls,
> Let them be black
> Or chocolate brown
> Or make them the

Colour of dust—
Dustlike
Browner than sand.
But if you can
Please keep them black,
Black. . . .

The Will to Power: A Study of Soyinka's Plays

M. PUSHPA

Power corrupts man. Opportunists wait for the right moment to snatch a chance, and make the most of it. This ailment is contagious, and effects the marrow of the society. It is like quicksands—it engulfs the victims. The road to power has many diversions and by-ways—through politics, academic skill, magic, traditional status, religion, affectation.

Kongi's Harvest and *A Play of Giants*[1] are a microcosm of the contemporary political situation, a situation relevant to Nigeria. The modern replacement for the traditional authority is also a kind of dictator. In *Kongi's Harvest* though Oba's power is curbed, his spiritual and moral grip is retained. Soyinka detested dictators and the brutality associated with them. The individuals have the power to find an escape route from this claustrophobic tyrannical rule. *Kongi's Harvest* delves deep into the problem of who is the ruler of Isma. Is it the traditional ruler Oba Danlola or the usurper Kongi, who is well-endowed with modern equipment and methods of coercion. Yet another contender is Daodu, the modern idealist whose recipe for good administration is a mixture of traditionalism and modernism. Soyinka's political vision attains clarity—for him the individual is important. His traumatic experiences as a victim of his country's military regime have left indelible scars on his psyche. Suppression of the rights of individuals is unpardonable for Soyinka. He respects a regime which recognizes an individual's right to sovereignty. The political web in *Kongi's Harvest* comprises many strands. The main strands are Kongi and Oba Danlola. Kongi, a champion of new values, wants to destroy the substratum of tradition. The Oba resists the onslaught of these modern forces. Autocrats like Kongi drunk with power destroy all those who cross their path. Daodu, the Oba's nephew, wants a rule which is a cross-fertilization of the traditional forces and the modernist forces. Daodu`s coup ends in a failure. Kongi is a typical example of a dictator, a brutal egoist, a man who has animalism of a man climbing the ladder to power. A blood-thirsty tyrant, he loves to prey on his people. His life is a publicity stunt—he fasts, but has no concern for the welfare of the people. Kongi and his men are trapped in a situation where to preserve their sanity, they use words and slogans as mere jargon. Kongi stands for denial of life, while Daodu stands for life. Daodu wants to overthrow Kongi. It is not an easy task to overthrow a well-entrenched autocrat. Daodu is a revolutionary, who has no patience for rituals.

Each of these characters is afflicted with the power syndrome. Intimations of immortality are a direct result of the mania for power. True power rests on humility and generosity. Egoism leads the protagonist nowhere. The pursuit of power leads them to an abysmal darkness, where there is nothing but destruction and self-annihilation.

Kongi's lust for power becomes a devouring passion. Daodu, on the other hand, is enhancing the quality of life through diligent cultivation of land. The play ends on a note of confusion. The indications are that the strife will continue.

> But
> Contented? That is one uneasy crown
> Which still eludes my willing head. (136)

A Play of Giants once again dwells on the dehumanizing power of politics. Kamini is a monstrosity who looms large in the play. He is a sadistic mass murderer. He is the dictator ruling over Bugara. The play is about the game of power involving all the giants of the African political scene. All of them are intoxicated with power, and do not want to accept any responsibility. Kamini has placed an order for a status. The sculptor jokingly comments that it is for the chamber of horrors. One sees a streak of sadism in his character. His ill-treatment of the sculptor is illustrative of his character.

The play deals with what is termed as "metaphysics of power." The corrupting power of men is a universal malady. Kamini's intention is to fill the country with mindless terror. In his zealous pursuit of dissolute power, he is embarrassed by his own personality decorated with medals. He is a sinister character, and a joker too. His thirst for power has reduced him to the depths of depravity. The essential link between responsibility and power is missing. The world is beset with power-mongers. The ruler in many countries is a dictator in modern clothes. Kamini is modelled on Idi Amin. He is in control of the situation all the time. He has no time for abstract issues—all that he wants is power.

Self-seeking individualism too, is one manifestation of the thirst for power. In *The Lion and the Jewel*, Baroka, the chieftain prevents any move for reform. He jealously guards his fortress. He is not against progress, but wants to establish his brand of progress. Baroka is intoxicated with power, and is keen on retaining his seat of power. Association of essential values of life is his trump card. He goes straight to the point while Lahunle gropes in the jungle of verbosity to express his thoughts and feelings. Leaning heavily on the bulwark of tradition, he maintains his supremacy. Exercise of power sustains him, and he spares no pains to keep this power with him.

Baroka's announcement of his impotency is a fine stroke of strategy. Sidi falls into the trap. She prefers Baroka to Lakunle, as he has strength of mind to be practical. Lakunle, 'the book-nourished shrimp' is a man lost in the maze of academic and bookish knowledge. His approach to life is stilted. Even in his romantic interludes, he lacks spontaneity. He is a walking dictionary, and lacks courage to be practical. Lakunle lacks affluence and situational advantages enjoyed by Baroka. The Bale is life-principle, the position he occupies has invested him with power which he can use indiscriminately. At sixty-two, he still retains his physical and mental agility which Lakunle lacks. Baroka can write the destiny of Ilujinle, and he has no hesitation in doing so. Through his sexual exploits and practical approach, he asserts his power.

Religious exploitation is yet another avenue which leads people to power. The protagonist Jeroboam in *The Trials of Brother Jero* is a beach prophet. He exploits the weakness of human beings, by being a glib talker appealing to their religious sentiments. Religion for him is a lucrative business. He exploits the credulous nature and emotional weakness of the people to gain his own ends. A self-confessed rogue, he made preaching his trade. He has a weakness for women though he deliberately avoids them. Brother Jeroboam represents the sick, materialistic nature of contemporary Nigeria. Jero is a typical power monger, whose actions represent a rupture between what he is and what he professes.

Jero has the ability to attract a large gathering of devotees. The people who gathered there are motivated by various ideas. No one has come for spiritual edification; they seek supernatural help in fulfilling their ambitions. Jero climbs up the ladder of power, using his gullible devotees as his foothold. Power seekers like Jero exploit sensitive situations to their advantage.

Brother Jero's transformation is seen in *Jero's Metamorphosis.* Once again he is a power-seeker, assuming the post of the leader of CASA (Church of the Apostolic Salvation Army). He explains to the Chief Executive Officer of the Tourist Board: "We are not fanatics. Our symbol is blood. It washes all sins away." (210) He strives for power, and his pursuit concludes with a stunning one-liner, "After all, it is the fashion these days to be a desk General." (213) He removes the photograph of the secular head of state, and replaces it with a larger one of himself. He claims monopoly of spiritual acumen.The transformed Jero is now eager to exploit the situation as much as possible. He uses Rebecca's services to steal the confidential file. He no longer seeks refuge in an ascetic facade; he enjoys the comfort of a business-line plush office of a general.

Jero plays are full of people who are engaged in mindless pursuits of materialism. These are power-seekers motivated by self-interest. Jones commented: "Jero, a professional survivalist, takes the measure of the wind accurately."[2] The society we see in these plays is one that existed during the period of transition. This period provides a chance for powermongers to flourish.

Power cannot be equated with ambition always. Igwezu in *The Swamp Dwellers* goes in search of prosperity in the city. He decides to make use of his talents and abilities to achieve what his brother has achieved. He is not a grabber, but aspires for a comfortable life. Olunde in *Death and King's Horseman* carries on the tradition of the Horseman committing suicide merely because he wants to preserve the unity of the society.

Man's situation on earth is such that he finds himself trapped in the cyclic pattern of life: of hope and despair. He depends on his will which becomes the propelling force of all action. Will is supreme, but the problem starts when it clashes with the social psyche. Soyinka did not tolerate the misuse of power. "I have a special responsibility, because I can smell the reactionary sperm years before the rape of the nation takes place."[3] Power should be co-ordinated with a sense of values which helps to maintain the line of demarcation between good and evil. The individual should have the capacity of providing a rampart against the force of evil.

War is a playground for power-mongers. In *Madmen and Specialists* we find the people physically maimed and mentally distorted. It is power sadism which leads the people on the wrong path. The Professor in *The Road* is a destroyer and a manipulator of road accidents. He is in search of the Word which will give him the power he yearns for. He dies, and we are not sure if he has deciphered the meaning of the Word.

Education enables a man to have a wider perspective of life. Olunde in *Death and the King's Horseman* has come out of the claustrophobic environs of self-interest. He does not view the rituals as a cluster of dogmatic values. The power-drive launched by the whites has to be crushed by an enlightened African. The ritual suicide is an offshoot of ageless wisdom—it is not the result of blind faith or superstition.

Man has the power to monitor the course of mankind, but this is misused by leaders and strong men. Their decisions are motivated by petty interests and selfish motives. The power of will is something which defies analysis sometimes. This will can lead man to prosperity, and sometimes to disastrous ends. Characters like the traditional African priest, beach preacher or political leaders exploit the credulity of people to enjoy the fruits of power.

Man is a product of his environment, and his response to the situation is of significance. "Society is a complex network of individualized incarnations of vital force and social participation is at bottom a complex of relationship between these."[4] An inflated love of power leads man astray. He becomes dehumanised and loses his sanity and mental equilibrium. A play like *Madmen and Specialists* depicts a world in which we see the power of evil. An individual should have the ability to protect his sensibility against these disruptive forces of society. A sad note in this well-orchestrated world of human emotion is the perversity of human mind.

Leaders and strong men are endowed with the power to change. These men have a tendency to direct their powers for personal aggrandizement. Such men become sadists and this power sadism can be very destructive. A strong will linked with a deep thirst for power can lead to disastrous ends. This spells doom for himself and the society. We would say with Soyinka:

> Time's Slaves
> Eunuchs of will, wait upon you.

NOTES

1. Wole Soyinka, *Collected Plays 1* (London: Oxford University Press, 1973) and *Collected Plays 2* (London: Oxford University Press, 1974).

2. E.D. Jones, *The Writing of Wole Soyinka* (London: Heinemann, 1983), p. 72.
3. James Gibbs, ed., *Critical Perspectives on Wole Soyinka* (London: Heinemann, 1981).
4. Abiola Irele, *The African Experience in Literature and Ideology* (Bloomington: Indiana University Press, 1990), p. 77.

Society in a State of Change: Wole Soyinka's *The Swamp Dwellers*

K. VENKATA REDDY

Generally, the plays of Wole Soyinka, like those of Bernard Shaw, are triggered off. *The Lion and the Jewel*, for instance, was triggered by Soyinka's reading about Charlie Chaplin's marriage at the age of nearly sixty to the teenaged Oona O'Neill. The news that oil had been found in marketable quantities in the Niger Delta prompted Soyinka to ponder over the impact of the access to sudden wealth on human relationships in a hitherto subsistence economy. The result was *The Swamp Dwellers* which was first performed by a group of young people at the Student Movement House, London, in September 1958, with Soyinka himself playing the role of its protagonist.[1] Small wonder, therefore, if the play bears the marks of Soyinka's academic background and displays only a few features of his characteristic style.

The Swamp Dwellers is concerned primarily with the social changes brought about by an easy access to sudden wealth. It demonstrates how easy money whatever may be its source, destroys.[2] The play comes to us essentially as an evocative study in disapppointment and frustration. Although its tone is graver than that of *The Lion and the Jewel*, it is "an examination of a society in a state of change."[3]

The Swamp Dwellers is set in a village of the Delta region of South-east Nigeria, an area in which farmable land is scarce, since it is periodically flooded with the waters of the river Niger. The members of the village belong to the Ijaw culture. Their lives are dominated by their observance of a local religion—the worship of the swamp Serpent. Although Soyinka does not specify the exact geographical location of the play, he does provide a very detailed description of the stage-set—a hut with its rush-baskets, 'adire' cloths and barber's equipment.The realistic presentation of the interior of the hut is enhanced by the sounds made by frogs and rain which suggest the swamps outside.

The play is about a poor couple, Makuri and Alu, and their twin sons, Awuchike and Igwezu. Ten years before the play opens, Awuchike had left for the city to seek his fortune and since then nothing has been heard of him. Igwezu, who had also gone to the city along with his wife for the same purpose some eight months ago, has returned to the village just then and has immediately rushed out to inspect his crops, "dashing off like a madman before anyone could ask him a thing." Alu, his mother, fears that he, like his brother, will go missing. Makuri dismissses her fears, making it clear that Igwezu knows the area too well to go lost. The husband and wife proceed to bicker over each other's weaknesses, until Alu takes offence and Makuri is forced to apologize and smooth over her bad temper by offering compliments. From the prolonged conversation of Makuri and Alu we learn that Igwezu is the owner of a farm in the swamps and that his harvest has been ruined by the floods.

The conversation of the couple is interrupted by the entrance of a blind beggar. He is tall, thin and a Muslim. We gather that he has come not to ask for charity, but to support himself by farming the land. He has travelled on foot from the north Nigeria to the Delta and he proposes to remain in the village and work there. He describes his personal history telling Makuri how he was blinded by fly-sickness as a child and how, having begun his career as a beggar, his conscience nagged at him for having accepted charity too casually and inadvertently from evil or irreligious men.

Again the conversation is interrupted, this time by the arrival of the Kadiye, the priest. Hearing that Igwezu has returned and anticipating that he had made his fortune in the city, the Kadiye visits Makuri's house and asks to be shaved by Igwezu, still absent from the hut, and promises to return after performing prayers over a circumcision.

Igwezu returns from his fields deeply shocked by the destruction of his farm. The Beggar assures Igwezu that his farm will thrive again and offers himself as his bondsman. He says: "I shall give myself to you and work the land for your good. I feel I can make it yield in my hands like an obedient child." (101) The Kadiye re-enters the hut and inquires of Igwezu how much money he has made in the city. Igwezu admits that he has actually gone into debt and before leaving the city he pledged the harvest from his farm as security for his debt. What is worse, it is his own brother, Awuchike, who has exacted this pledge from him. What is worse still, his wife has deserted him and has become his brother's mistress. The Kadiye gets ready for shave seating himself in the swivel chair.

While shaving the Kadiye, Igwezu quizzes him with a series of riddles and pours out a stream of questions about the responsibility of the Kadiye as priest of the Serpent. He points out that he has provided the Kadiye with all the valuable gifts that were required for the health of his farm and his marriage and demands to know why both his farm and his marriage have been destroyed. At one moment he seems sufficiently angry to slice into the rolls of fat beneath the priestly chin, but he restrains himself and allows the terrified Kadiye to scamper away. Appalled at his son's blasphemy, Makuri warns him that the Kadiye may not stir up the village against him. Sensing the danger Igwezu flees to the city advising the Beggar to remain in the village and cultivate the land. To the Beggar's question whether he will return, he gives no answer. The Beggar decides to stay on in the village "to give account." (112)

The ending of *The Swamp Dwellers* has come in for a good deal of criticism. The general feeling is that the play does not end on a positive note by showing the villagers casting off their superstitions and marching off to construct dykes and increase the amount of land available for farming.[5] James Gibbs questions: "What Soyinka wished to convey by his ending of *The Swamp Dwellers* is not absolutely clear: it is an ambiguous coda."[6] But a close look at the ending of the play provides a clue to Soyinka's technique of closing the play not by offering a solution to the problem presented in the play but by suggesting a 'new beginning' or a moment of temporary quiet after explosions of emotional tension.

The play comes to a close with the Beggar's final speech uttered by way of suggestively answering his own question put to Igwezu—"But you will return, master?"—as the latter walks off slowly. The Beggar says:

> The swallows find their nest again when the cold is over. Even the bats desert dark holes in the trees and flap wet leaves with wings of leather. There were wings everywhere as I wiped my feet against your threshold. I heard the cricket scratch himself beneath the armpit as the old man said to me. . . . I shall be here to give account. (112)

The speech, together with the stage image which accompanies it, suggests that Igwezu will return. The swallows provide a pattern which the young man may follow. Just as the swallows return to their nest when the cold is over, Igwezu will return home when his problems are solved. As the curtain falls, the Beggar becomes almost a statue—an encouraging presence, a man of integrity, a figure who embodies some hope for the future.

The Swamp Dwellers is a neatly structured play with a good beginning, a middle and an end. The structure of the play consists of the steady accumulation of details as each fresh entrance in the play admits further information. The narrative emerges through a variety of exchanges and we must be quite attentive in order to piece it together. The discussion of the elderly couple centring round the whereabouts of their twin sons constitutes the beginning. The middle is provided by the episode of the Beggar. Igwezu's encounter with the Kadiye touching on the priest's false promises and bad conduct forms the end.

The Swamp Dwellers maintains the three Unities closely. The play opens just before dusk and comes to a close after it gets dark, taking for its duration not more than two hours, almost the same time that is required for its enactment on the stage. The whole action takes place in Makuri's hut into which come a succession of visitors. The various strands of action—Awuchike's ingratitude to his parents and brother, the story of the blind Beggar, the betrayal of the trust of the villagers including Igwezu by the Kadiye—are unified into an organic whole by way of interlinking the incidents and inter-relating the characters. The various experiences of the Beggar, the Kadiye and Igwezu are closely related to each other.

The theatrical effectivenesss of the play is enhanced by the elements of surprise and suspense introduced by Soyinka skilfully mostly through the artistic manipulation of entrances and exits of characters. The charcacters tend to enter and leave the stage in succession. Through having the Kadiye enter, then exit and then enter again, and through having Igwezu arrive in between the two visits of the Kadiye the dramatist ensures that only gradually are all the characters brought together on stage at the same time. Accompanied by the drummer and the servant, the Kadiye's appearance on each occasion is striking and spectacular. Igwezu arrives from his farm silently without the notice of his parents. Alu's gasp of surprise when she does notice him is dramatically effective. Furthermore, Makuri's and Alu's anticipation of Igwezu's arrival leads them to mistake first the sound of the Beggar's footsteps, then the sound of the Kadiye's drumming, for their son's approach thereby rousing a good deal of suspense among the audience.

The Swamp Dwellers could be regarded as a drama of revelation. Very little actually happens in the play in terms of physical action. Virtually all the main events, except Igwezu's exposure of the Kadiye, have occurred by the time the action of the play begins. The opening conversation between Makuri and Alu reveals the history of the absence of their two sons. We learn that the son, Igwezu, who has returned, had a wife whom he took to the city on her insistence. Makurti reveals that Igwezu is the owner of a farm and that his crops have been ruined by floods. And with the Beggar's entrance at this point with his revelation of the loss of his crops to locusts and his search for land to cultivate, another strand is introduced in the gradual accumulation of facts. Thus, the process continues until all the characters are on stage and make their final revelations, the most shocking revelations being Igwezu's narration of his going into debt, his pledging of his harvest as security for his debt to no other than his own brother in the city and, what is worse, the desertion of him by his own wife who has become his brother's mistress. The revelations about various experiences and disappointments of different characters make an emotional impact upon the audience. To all the characters in general, and to Igwezu in particular, revelation means education and the means with which to respond critically to the gross corruption of the priest.

The Swamp Dwellers is essentially a play of mood and atmosphere, providing the audience with ample opportunity to make comparisons and reach their own judgments. Soyinka drives home to us the mood and atmosphere of the play mainly through implied contrasts, a technique that he generally employs in his plays for artistic purposes.

The most obvious contrast in the play is that between the twin brothers, Awuchike and Igwezu. They look alike but they behave very differently. Though Awuchike does not appear in person in the play, we learn of him only through Igwezu. Ruthless and heartless, Awuchike is a typical representative of a new class of Nigeria who has rejected the village, and all traditional ties of kinship in his inhuman accumulation of wealth. He has buried himself in the city and has sacrificed the responsibilities of family ties for success in the city. Igwezu, on the other hand, likes the village life and remains loyal to his home. His first act as soon as he has made a little fortune in the city is to send his father a barber's chair which he had promised when he left home. He would never have gone to the city but for the insistence of his wife. When he loses his fortune and wife in the city, his first thought is to return to his village and devote himself to his farm.

The two women in the family—Igwezu's mother and his wife—are also sharply contrasted. The weakness and infidelity of Igwezu's wife provide a contrast to the strength and virtue of his mother. Despite temptations from visiting traders, Alu had remained faithful to her husband. Similarly, the mutual understanding and affection between the old couple, Makuri and Alu, despite their bickering and finding fault with each other, contrasts itself with the awful lack of the same between the young couple, Igwezu and his wife.

The poor blind Beggar, a 'tall and thin' Muslim, possessing a fine 'ebony-carving' face, and a bearing of 'quiet dignity' falls a striking contrast to the rich Kadiye, a prosperous figure, big and voluminous with his fingers heavily ringed. Though a devout Muslim, the Beggar denies the religious value of begging, insisting as he does on a scheme of self-help that leads him to search for land which he can farm. A man of quick intelligence, he is able to analyze the ills of the society of the swamp dwellers and, what is more, offers encouragement to Igwezu when he turns against the false priest. The Beggar is "Christ-like in that he enters a hidebound traditional society and makes men begin to think again."[7] He gives himself selflessly and unasked for the good of others.

The Kadiye, on the other hand, is essentially a corrupt and self-centred person. A priest by profession, he is anything but pious. Worldly to the core, he is more concerned with the fortune that Igwezu might have made in the city than with his loss of his crops. He betrays the trust of the villagers by encouraging them to indulge in a meaningless cult. He does so not because he himself genuinely believes in it, but because it affords him the means of extorting their produce for his selfish ends. However we need not agree with Gerald Moore who says that the Kadiye is little more than a grotesque stage villain.[8] A close study of the play reveals how the Kadiye is refreshingly resourceful and a dramatically realized and convincing character.

The final contrast between the bitter hopelessness of Igwezu and the calm confidence of the Beggar react in different ways to their respective disasters. Igwezu's reference to the loss of his harvest is fraught with hopelessness. Almost in a wailing tone he says: "I have had my feast of welcome. I found it on the farm when the beans and the corn had made an everlasting potage with the mud." (101) Thus, Igwezu's mood is one of despair. But the Beggar has not lost hope and is in no way bitter. On the contrary, he insists on being allowed to cultivate the land: "I wish to work on the soil. I wish to knead it between my fingers." (89) Thus, the parallel disasters suffered by Igwezu and the Beggar are reacted by them in sharp contrast with one another. No doubt, Igwezu has shaken off the old shackles but he still has to work out, something as positive as the Beggar's resolute search for a new life.

Though Soyinka does not greatly vary his language in *The Swamp Dwellers*, as he does in other plays, particularly in *The Trials of Brother Jero*, to suggest distinctions between one character and another, the language is crisp and evocative, with effective use of proverbs. The dialogue contains powerful dramatic expression fashioned out of contemporary Nigerian English. To cite an instance, Igwezu says: "The city reared itself in the air, and with the strength of its legs of brass kicked the adventurer in the small of his back." (104) Another instance could be the Beggar's closing comments: "The swallows find their nest again when the cold is over. Even the bats desert dark holes in the trees and flap wet leaves with wings of leather." (112)

The Swamp Dwellers appears to have been modelled on the plays of Synge in general, and on his *Riders to the Sea* in particular, especially in its realistic presentation of a location—a typical village in the delta region of south-east Nigeria. As in Aran Islands which form the background of *Riders to the Sea*, the precarious living eked out by Igwezu is characteristic of an area in which farmable land is scarce. Although the setting and details of *The Swamp Dwellers* are local, the play, with some modifications, could be transposed to India or Ireland without impairing its meaning. It admirably suits the Indian rural background which is constantly subject to floods or drought, playing havoc with the lives of poor farmers like Igwezu. While witnessing the play, the Indian audience would feel at home and enjoy it as much, if not more, as the Nigerian audience. What more could be a proof of the universality of its themes and vision!

NOTES

1. Soyinka spoke about the 'genesis' of *The Swamp Dwellers* and other plays at a play-making workshop held in Harare during Decemebr 1981.
2. The experience of the oil-boom years in Nigeria showed this too clearly.
3. Eldred Durosimi Jones, *The Writing of Wole Soyinka* (London: Heinemann, 1973), p. 17.
4. Wole Soyinka, *Collected Plays*, (Oxford: Oxford University Press, 1973), vol. I, p. 82.
5. "Three Views of *The Swamp Dwellers*," *Ibadan Magazine* (June 1959), pp. 27-30.
6. James Gibbs, *Wole Soyinka*, p. 44.
7. Eldred Jones, p. 19.
8. Gerald Moore. *Wole Soyinka* (London: Evans, 1978), p. 42.

The Conflict between Tradition and Modernity in Wole Soyinka's *The Lion and the Jewel*

BASAVARAJ S. NAIKAR

The conflict between tradition and modernity is the central thematic concern of Wole Soyinka's *The Lion and the Jewel*.[1] A deft comedy which provides excellent theatre to the audience, it draws heavily on the theme of colonial conflict. The main characters of this comedy can be classified into two groups: Baroka, Sadiku and Sidi represent the traditional African values whereas Lakunle stands for modern European, especially British values of life. The conflict between the two value-systems is triggered off by the germination of amorous love between Sidi, a beautiful young girl of about sixteen years and Lakunle, a young school teacher in Ilujinle. As is natural for a young man, Lakunle is infatuated with Sidi as the latter happens to be a pretty young girl in the African village. When Sidi is passing through the lane near the school, Lakunle chances to see her and begins to express his appreciation of her beauty and a special concern for her well-being. As he sees her carrying a pot of water on her head, he feels anxious for her and therefore, advises her:

> I have told you not to carry loads
> On your head. But you are as stubborn
> As an illiterate goat. It is bad for your spine.
> And it shortens your neck, so that very soon
> You will have no neck at all. Do you wish to look
> Squashed like my pupils' drawings? (4)

He taunts her by saying that "Only spiders/Carry loads the way you do." (4) He advises her to cover up her chest thereby discouraging the idlers of the village. Lakunle's initial infatuation matures into his desire to marry Sidi. When she asks him for her pail which he has snatched away from her, he lays the condition: "Not till you swear to marry me." (7) He also explains to her why he wants to marry her. He thinks her to be an intelligent girl who can understand him and, therefore, support him in his struggle for life:

> (Takes her hand, instantly soulful)
> Sidi, a man must prepare to fight alone.
> But it helps if he has a woman
> To stand by him, a woman who . . .
> Can understand . . . like you. (7)

Lakunle tries to court the village belle because he believes in the modern European concept of love finally resulting in marriage. It is here that the crux of the problem lies. Though Lakunle is an African by birth, he has Europeanised himself by his modern education and contact with the alien culture. In fact he has acculturated himself to the extent that he has imbibed the values of European culture. But Sidi remains a traditional girl to the core. She believes in the orthodox African values of life, including the conventions of marriage. She, therefore, does not believe in the European concept of 'love marriage.' She expects him to buy her by giving her bride-price:

> I have told you, and I say it again
> I shall marry you today, next week
> Or any day you name.
> But my bride-price must first be paid.
> Aha, now you turn away.
> But I tell you Lakunle, I must have
> The full bride-price. Will you make me
> A laughing stock? Well, do as you please.
> But Sidi will not make herself
> A cheap bowl for the village spit. (8)

Lakunle, who has learnt the European ways of life, does not subscribe to the traditional African customs of marriage. He, therefore, does not want to pay any bride-price to the girl he is going to marry. Payment of bride-price will be tantamount to buying a piece of property:

> Ignorant girl, can you not understand?
> To pay the price would be

To buy a heifer off the market stall.
You'd be my chattel, my mere property.
No, Sidi! (Very tenderly) (9)

There is a striking difference between the two about the bride-price. Sidi has her own reasons for insisting upon the bride-price. Should she marry him without the bride-price, the traditional society will cast aspersion on her sexual purity:

They will say I was no virgin
That I was forced to sell my shame
And marry you without a price. (8)

Apart from the controversy about bride-price, there is also a striking difference between them in the purpose of marriage and in life-styles. Lakunle wishes to marry her more for companionship than for the traditional purpose of procreation. He looks down upon the African customs:

An ignoble custom, infamous, ignominous
Shaming our heritage before the world.
Sidi, I do not seek a wife
To fetch and carry
To cook and scrub,
To bring forth children by the gross. (8-9)

On the contrary, he wishes to marry her as he wants her to be a 'life-companion,' 'a friend in need/ And an equal partner in my race of life.'

Sidi does not agree with him. A believer in the traditional values of life, she considers child-bearing a sacred part of matrimony. She, therefore, asks him:

Heaven forgive you!
Do you now scorn
Child-bearing in a wife? (9)

They differ in their views about kissing also. Lakunle considers it 'a way of civilized romance' and requests her to give him a kiss:

Be a modern wife, look me in the eye
And give me a little kiss—like this.
(Kisses her) (10)

Sidi does not like it because she looks at it from the African point of view. She considers it rather unhygienic:

> No, don't! I tell you I dislike
> This strange unhealthy mouthing you perform. (10)

Sidi, thus, does not show any appreciation of Lakunle's modern, European or Christian ways of loving or marrying. Nor does she show any special liking for him, his youth or his intellectual abilities.

Meanwhile something interesting happens in her life. The European and mechanical amenities help her to have an unprecedented confidence in her. For example, a European comes riding his 'new horse' (motor cycle) into the village. He has brought with him a 'one-eyed box' (camera). He has taken the snapshots of many villagers including Sidi and published these in a 'book' (magazine). Sidi who has seen her own photograph beautifully printed on the front cover of the magazine, develops a new confidence about her youthful beauty. She develops a bloated egoism about herself especially when her attention is drawn to the fact that Baroka's "image is in a little corner somewhere in the book, and even that corner he shares with one of the village latrines." (12) The wide advertisement given to her beauty by the European means i.e. camera and magazine, Sidi grows so proud that she begins to look down upon even Baroka, the lion of Ilujinle. She expresses her pride playfully before Lakunle:

> Well, don't you know?
> Sidi is more important even than Bale.
> More famous than the panther of the trees.
> He is beneath me now—
> Your fearless rake, the courage of womanhood!
> But now,
> He shares the corner of the leaf
> With the lowest of the low—
> With the dug-out village latrine! (13)

Sidi's pride of beauty makes her refuse the request of Baroka who wants to marry her as his juniormost and latest wife. After her beauty is proved beyond doubt by the colourful photograph in the magazine, she does not want any certificate from anybody:

My name is Sidi. And now, let me be.
My name is Sidi, and I am beautiful.
The stranger took my beauty
And placed it in my hands.
Here, here it is. I need no funny names
To tell me of my fame.
Loveliness beyond the jewel of a throne—
That is what he said. (20)

She thinks that she is desired by men like Baroka only after her beauty is publicized in the magazine:

Why did the Lion not bestow his gift
Before my face was lauded to the world? (20)

In her opinion, her beauty would add to the pride of Baroka:

Baroka merely seeks to raise his manhood
Above my beauty.
He seeks new fame
As the one man who has possessed
The jewel of Ilujinle! (21)

She has other reservations also about Baroka. His old age happens to be one of the hindrances in her possible alliance with him:

He's old. I never knew till now,
He was that old. (21)

The new awareness of her beauty makes her almost blind to others's point of view. She grows narcissistic about her physical charm:

To think I took
No notion of my velvet skin.
How smooth it is!
And no man ever thought
To praise the fullness of my breasts. (21)

Her narcissistic awareness of beauty makes her look down upon men who seek her hand in marriage. She has no respect for the intellectual achievements of Lakunle and, therefore, nicknames him as a 'book-worm.' She contrasts her own superiority with Baroka's inferiority:

> See how the water glistens on my face
> Like the dew-moistened leaves on a Harmattan morning.
> But he—his face is like a leather piece
> Torn rudely from the saddle of his horse
> (Sadiku gasps)
> Sprinkled with the musty ashes
> From a pipe that is long over-smoked.
> And this goat-like tuft
> Which I once thought was manly;
> It is like scattered twists of grass;
> Not even green—
> But charred and lifeless, as after a forest fire!
> Sadiku, I am young and brimming; he is spent.
> I am the twinkle of a jewel,
> But he is the hind quarters of a lion! (22)

It is precisely for this reason that she refuses to marry him. Sadiku, the senior wife of Baroka, notices Sidi's adamance. She changes her strategy and requests Sidi to go and have supper at Baroka's home. Sidi, who is very smart, sees through the wiles of Baroka. She flatly refuses to sup with married men, as she very well knows the consequences:

> Can you deny that
> Every woman who has supped with him one night,
> Becomes his wife or concubine the next? (23)

Sadiku is nonplussed by Sidi's pointblank refusal to Baroka's proposal. When Sadiku conveys the same to Baroka, he also feels insulted and embarrassed. For a little while he does not know what to do to attract Sidi into his bed. Then he hits upon a clever plan and pretends to have lost his virility:

> The time has come when I can fool myself
> No more. I am no man, Sadiku. My manhood
> Ended near a week ago. (27-28)

He explains to Sadiku why he wants to have a young wife like Sidi:

I wanted Sidi because I still hoped
A foolish thought I know, but still—I hoped
That, with a virgin young and hot within,
My failing strength would rise and save my pride. (28)

He pretends impotence, thereby giving an artificial satisfaction to Sadiku. He sends the latter to plead again with Sidi to become his wife. Sadiku employs a new technique of weaning Sidi to her husband's bed, by misleading her about the whole issue. She tells Sidi that it is now time for women to rejoice over their victory over men who have lost their virility. Sidi is not able to see through the wiles of Sadiku when the latter invites her to participate in a ritual: "The scarecrow is here. Begone fop! This is the world of women. At this moment our star sits in the centre of the sky. We are supreme. What is more, we are about to perform a ritual. If you remain, we will chop you up, we will make you the sacrifice." (31) Sadiku further arouses Sidi's curiosity by stating that it is only women who are allowed to watch the ritual and not men. This kind of prohibition for men further appetises Sidi's curiosity. Sadiku uses the resourceful wiles of her sex in such a subtle fashion that Sidi develops an irresistible urge to participate in the ritual and mock at the 'impotence' of Baroka:

Stop, Sadiku stop. Oh such an idea
Is running in my head. Let me to the palace for
This supper he promised me. Sadiku, what a way
To mock the devil. (32)

Sidi wants to enjoy teasing Baroka about his loss of manliness:

Oh Sadiku let me go.
I long to see him thwarted, to watch his longing,
His twitching hands which this time cannot
Rush to loosen his trouser cords. (32)

Banking upon the gullibility of Sidi, Sadiku goads her further: "You will have to match the fox's cunning. Use your bashful looks and be truly repentant. Goad him my child, torment him until he weeps for shame." (32)

Brainwashed and misled by Sadiku in addition to her own bloated and narcissistic ego, Sidi does not listen to Lakunle's precautionary words. She meets Baroka in privacy, but is finally deflowered by the virile man of sixty. Sadiku is very happy to note that she has succeeded in her trick of fooling Sidi and causing the latter's loss of virginity. But Lakunle feels hurt to see his beloved deflowered by his rival. Yet his liberal outlook enables him to forgive Sidi for her loss of virginity and offer to marry her. But Sidi who has experienced sexual joy with Baroka refuses to marry Lakunle:

> Marry who . . . ? You thought . . .
> Did you really think that you, and I . . .
> Why, did you think that after him,
> I could endure the touch of another man?
> I who have felt the strength,
> The perpetual youthful zest
> Of the panther of the trees?
> And would I choose a watered-down,
> A beardless version of an unripened man? (57)

She further eulogizes Baroka's sexual strength which has given her a new lease of life:

> Out of my way, book-nourished shrimp.
> Do you see what strength he has given me?
> That was not bad. For a man of sixty,
> It was the secret of God's own draught
> A deed for drums and ballads.
> But you, at sixty, you'll be ten years dead!
> In fact, you'll not survive your honeymoon . . .
> Come to my wedding if you will. If not . . . (57)

The final surrender of Sidi to Baroka is evidence of the victory of traditional African values over the modern, European ones in the African context. Sadiku is very happy about the success of her trick in pushing Sidi into Baroka's bed. She and her husband do not believe in the importance of sex for itself. On the contrary, they respect sex for its procreative purposes. That is the reason why she blesses Sidi: "May the time come soon when you shall be as round-bellied as a full moon in a low sky." Sidi also has accepted the sanctity of procreative sex and virility of Baroka. She, therefore, says:

Come, sing to me of seeds
Of children, sired of the lion-stock. (57)

The conflict between African values and modern European values is ultimately resolved in favour of the former. Lakunle, in spite of his European ways of life, is looked down upon and finally rejected by Sidi who conforms to African tradition by marrying Baroka. Sidi who had at least jokingly considered Baroka as equal to her father in age has finally accepted him as her bed-mate and life-partner. Conversely, Baroka who used to address Sidi as a 'child' or a 'daughter' has finally initiated her into the unforgettable joys of matrimonial sex.

One may easily see the contrast between traditional African value-system and modern European value-system. Compared to the African conventions of marriage like payment of bride-price, Lakunle's modern European way of loving a woman to marry her are not accepted by the people like Baroka. Compared to the cunning ways of drawing a young lady into bed, Lakunle's rational method of convincing a young lady into accepting the marriage-proposal is not appreciated by the tradition-ridden Sidi. Compared to the animalistic, functional and powerful sexual pleasure offered to Sidi by Baroka, Lakunle's aesthetics of love and poetic sensibility have no significance in the tradition-ridden society.

Modernity is defeated by tradition not only in the case of marriage between Sidi and Baroka, but in other social matters as well. For example, when the surveyer comes to Ilujinle to cut down the forest and lay the railway track, the Bale of Ilujinle feels that the integrity of the country is threatened. Lakunle describes Baroka as the enemy of modernity or progress:

My father told me, before he died. And few men
Know of this trick—oh he's a die-hard rogue
Sworn against our progress . . . yes it was somewhere here,
The track should have been laid just along
The outskirts. Well, the workers came, in fact
It was prisoners who were brought to do
The harder part . . . to break the jungle's back. (24)

The laying of the railway track would have helped the people of Ilujinle to enter into the network of international trade, civilization and communication. But Baroka, who is an enemy of such progress or modernity, avoided the laying of the said track by bribing the surveyer with a wad of pound notes, kola nuts and a coop of hens. Lakunle thus points out how old-fashioned Baroka is. The paradox is that the old-fashioned Bale is powerful enough to avoid the entry of modern civilization into the heart of traditional Africa.

Lakunle dreams of the entry of civilization or modernity into Africa very soon through the construction of a motor road. He believes, rather wishfully, that there would be a remarkable change in the life-style of the villagers. He gives a contrastive picture of the traditional and the modernized Africa. He believes that the conventional bride-price would be cancelled and replaced by the simple method of love-marriage; that the motor-road would connect the village to urban life; that clay pots would be replaced by saucepans; that polygamy would be replaced by monogamy; that the forests would be cut down and replaced by modern parks for the benefit of lovers; that palm wine habit would be replaced by tea with milk and sugar; that they would publish their own newspapers, build new factories and send their girls for beauty contests. Lakunle wants to educate his beloved but the latter is not attracted by his fashionable ideas at all. He wants the people of the village to enjoy the amenities of industrialization. He assures Sidi:

> But don't you worry. In a year or two
> You will have machines which will do
> Your pounding, which you will grind your pepper
> Without it getting into your eyes. (6)

These advantages are looked down upon as absurd by Sidi who accuses him:

> O-oh. You really mean to turn
> The whole world upside down. (6)

An important contrast might be noticed between the traditional African culture and the modern or Europeanized way of life with regard to love or courting. Lakunle, for example, believes in addressing his beloved in a very poetic language. He describes how he would like to behave with her after marrying her:

> When we are wed, you shall not walk or sit
> Tethered as it were, to my dirtied heels
> Together we shall sit at table

—Not on the floor—and eat,
Not with fingers, but with knives
And forks, and breakable plates
Like civilized beings.
I will not have you wait on me
Till I have dined my fill.
No wife of mine, no lawful wedded wife
Shall eat the leavings off my plate—
That is for the children.
I want to walk beside you in the street,
Side by side and arm in arm
Just like the Lagos couples I have seen
High-heeled shoes for the lady, red paint
On her lips. And her hair is stretched
Like a magazine photo. I will teach you
The waltz and we'll learn the foxtrot
And we'll spend the weekend in night clubs at Ibadan.
Oh I must show you the grandeur of towns
We'll live there if you like or merely pay visits.
So choose. Be a modern wife, look me in the eye
And give me a little kiss—like this.
(Kisses her) (9)

His words not only show his poetic and romantic sensibility and his dream of a modern matrimonial life, but also provide a sharp contrast to the traditional African life. Being an educated man, he has filled his head with many new ideas. He dreams of translating them into action one day. But the African way of life is diametrically opposed to Lakunle's dream of modernity. Baroka, for example, is an embodiment of African life-style. Being an uneducated man, he has no books or new ideas. Nor has he a poetic heart or romantic sensibility. He does not believe in attracting the attention of women by appealing to their heart or poetic sensibility. Nor does he enjoy noticing the beauty of women's bewitching limbs. His illiterate indifference to women's beauty is amply expressed in his words to Sidi:

Now that
Is a question which I never thought to hear
Except from a school teacher. Do you think
The Lion has such leisure that he asks

The whys and wherefores of a woman's
Squint? (38)

Baroka's interest in women or sex has not even an iota of aesthetic touch. On the contrary, it is blatantly animalistic and shamelessly functional. That is the reason why he says:

I change my wrestlers when I have learnt
To throw them. I also change my wives
When I have learnt to tire them. (39)

Sidi's approach to life is complementary to Baroka's. Being deeply rooted in the African tradition, she is not attracted by Lakunle's Europeanized and sophisticated approach to life. Her philosophy perfectly matches Baroka's animalistic and vitalistic one. That is the reason why she is magnetically attracted to him after tasting his virility in bed. She refuses to marry Lakunle precisely for that reason. This phenomenon testifies to the deep-rooted strength of tradition unshaken by the superficial wind of Europeanization or modernity.

There is a sharp contrast between the African viewpoint and the European one with regard to 'progress.' Whereas Lakunle and kindred souls believe in the European ideas of progress expressed in terms of their belief in the establishment of roads, rails and bridges and introduction of industry and technology in various aspects of life, which would shorten the distance between people of different countries by bringing them into the wide network of communication and transportation and by rendering their life more comfortable. But the African point of view as expressed through Baroka's opinions, does not agree with the modern point of view. Baroka expresses his opinion very clearly:

For a long time now,
The town-dwellers have made up tales
Of the backwardness of Ilujinle
Until it hurts Baroka, who holds
The welfare of his people deep at heart. . . .
I do not hate progress, only its nature
Which makes all the roofs and faces look the same. (47)

In Baroka's view, the so-called progress not only contributes to the mechanical uniformity of things, but also suppresses the elemental vitality and beauty of Nature. He, therefore, says:

> Among the bridges and the murderous roads,
> Below the humming birds which
> Smoke the face of Sango, dispenser of
> The snake-tongue lightning, between this moment
> And the reckless broom that will be wedded
> In these years to come, we must leave
> Virgin plots of lives, rich decay
> And the tang of vapour rising from
> Forgotten heaps of compost, lying
> Undisturbed. . . . But the skin of progress
> Masks, unknown, the spotted wolf of sameness . . .
> Does sameness not revolt your being
> My daughter? (47-48)

Such views held by Baroka, obviously, show the fact that modernity is not always desirable and that the native, rural, traditional culture has its own vitality and beauty which needs to be discovered by the people. Baroka's respect for his own culture does not allow him to recognize the so-called superiority of Western culture. Lakunle's modernity and Europeanization are proportionate to the process of his own acculturation.

The final triumph of African tradition over modernity and Westernization is obviously an objective correlative of Wole Soyinka's philosophy which recognizes the postcolonial need for nativization or reculturation and rediscovery of the past glory and grandeur. Gerald Moore rightly says that "the surprise ending of *The Lion and the Jewel* presents a substantial moral—'Man, be thyself.'"[2] Soyinka's lesson is, obviously, a model for all the postcolonial writers of the world.

NOTES

1. Wole Soyinka, *The Lion and the Jewel* in *Collected Plays* (London: Oxford University Press, 1974).
2. Gerald Moore, *Twelve African Writers* (London: Hutchinson, 1983), p. 221.

Wole Soyinka's *A Dance of the Forests*

A.P. DANI

A Dance of the Forests, a play performed as part of the Nigerian Independence Celebrations in October 1960, is one of the landmarks in Soyinka's career as a man of letters, the others being *The Road, Kongi's Harvest, The Interpreters* (1965) *Idanre and Other Poems* (1967). The play "denigrated the glorious African past and warned Nigerians and all Africans that their energies henceforth should be spent trying to avoid repeating the mistakes that have already been made."

By the early 1960s Soyinka had been recognized as an important dramatist. His apprenticeship at the Royal Court Theatre at the time of the rebirth of British drama with playwrights like Beckett, Osborne, Arden and Wesker and his study and research in traditional African drama have considerably influenced his plays. They reveal "a fusion of local traditional Yoruba dramatic forms and more universal influences. In the Yoruba folk opera we have the following elements: a poetic language working through image and allusion, music that talks with and to the performers, dance to express and comment upon characters and events and themes drawn from the culture and experience of the audience. Soyinka calls this as a "people's theatre" appropriately. He has always been a supporter of the Yoruba folk opera playwrights in their attitude towards language. As a Yoruba, even writing in English, he is conscious of the rich possibilities of allusion and is constantly referring back to details of Yoruba folk love and custom. A non-Yoruba reader or audience might find Soyinka a little baffling. His use of language is evocative and the playwright calls upon the experience, beliefs, fantasies and emotions of his audience. In the folk opera, the language is paralleled by the music and dance, often using traditional dance steps or particular musical statements that are vivid in themselves, perhaps steps used for a certain ceremony or by the worshippers of a particular god. The basic elements of the traditional Nigerian theatre viz. music and dance have been incorporated by Soyinka into the European theatrical forms. Soyinka as a satirical writer comments upon the universal themes such as the frailty of power seekers in his plays like *A Dance of the Forests, Kongi's Harvest* and *The Road* where dance and music have been used fully. The enlivened language, the clarity of movement and the comment of the music find new powers in the theatre.

There are two broad groups of Nigerian drama, namely, the traditional, which includes the sacred and the secular drama and the modern, in which one finds the folks theatre and the literary drama. However, music, dance and poetry have been associated with Nigerian drama from the earliest birth, marriage and death cycle ceremonies and rituals to the present trials by error of today. The traditional theatre of sacred and secular plays indicated a unified combination of the arts. This composite art of the folk theatre is noticed in the literary plays of Soyinka.

A good knowledge of Yoruba religious mythology is of great importance to the understanding of Soyinka's works. For example, Ogun, a Yoruba God, is shown as a human being and as a god. Ogun is presented as fiery and destructive as well as kind and protective. In *A Dance of the Forests*, the duality of Ogun's character (destructiveness and creativity) is already appreciated but the emphasis is on the negative side. Soyinka's major interest in Ogun is to illustrate that human nature is unpredictable, ambivalent and unreliable. The situation of man on earth is such that he is tied to a cyclical pattern of life and death, of hope and despair. In such a situation man has sought guidance from higher beings but these beings have proved very inadequate in tackling man's problems. The gods do not seem to have a rational mode of manifestation. They cannot be relied upon to settle human affairs. Man should depend upon his will in facing his problems without necessarily abandoning the gods entirely. But man's will could and occasionally does lead him to misplaced adventures, unanticipated ends, and downright silly antics and untold cruelties. All the same, human will must always be the propelling force behind human action. Without it the world will be unmitigatedly tragic.

"I who await a mother/Feel this dread I'll be born dead" cries the half child in *A Dance of the Forest*. The half-child is Nigeria. Even now Soyinka's fears for Nigeria's stability and political sanity remain acute. The horror of being stillborn is experienced by many of his characters, for if the nations's fate is fractured and chaotic, so will be the lives of its people. How an individual can negotiate a path of decency and principle in a modern African state is one of his major concerns. The past will not help him to solve his problems. Adenebi, the Council Orator's high hopes are ruined at the court of Mata Kharibu where he was Court Historian. The Warrior (the Captain) who is the Dead Man tells the Physician: "I took up soldiering to defend my country, but those to whom I gave the power to command my life abuse my trust in them." The Historian Adenebi tells Mata Kharibu: "War is the only consistency the past ages afford us. It is the legacy which new nations seek to perpetuate. Patriots are grateful for wars. Soldiers have never questioned bloodshed. The cause is always the accident your Majesty, and war is the Destiny." He further argues: "history has always revealed that the soldier who will not fight has the blood of slaves in him. The Dead Woman tells Demoke: "A hundred generations have made no difference."

The Forest Head desires to lay out the rites of the dead but he realizes that it is futile "to bear the mirror of original nakedness." But he must persist knowing that nothing is altered. The only hope he has is that when he has "tortured awareness from their souls" that is the new beginning.

From the testimony of Aroni, the Lame One, we learn that the Dead ones desired to have their illustrious ancestors present at the Feast, the Gathering of the Tribes, where the Forests would dance for them. The Forest Head Obaneji, Demoke, the Carver (Poet in the Court of Mata Kharibu) and Rola, a whore known as Madame Tortoise for centuries, would also participate in the dance. It was not a dignified dance. Eṣhuoro, a wayward cult-spirit, cried for vengeance and stratagems. Ogun, the patron god of carvers, protects carvers, smiths and all workers in iron though he is often associated with the battlefield. Murete tells Aroni: "He [Agboreko, Elder of Sealed Lips] said they asked Forest father for illustrious ancestors and you sent them accusers."

Obaneji refers to the history of the lorry which involved a lot of corruption. The lorry met with an accident and out of seventy people on board only five escaped. Obaneji wants Adenebi to give him the name of the persons who took the bribe for record's sake. When Adenebi accuses him with insensitivity, Obaneji retorts: "I didn't kill them. And anyway we have our different views. The world must go on. After all, what are a mere sixty-five souls burnt to death? Nothing, your bribe taker was only a small-time murderer, he wasn't even cold-blooded. He doesn't really interest me very much."

The expression vividly brings out the unfeeling and callous manifestation of human corruption. Aroni, as Ageborko maintains, is Wisdom itself. When Aroni means to expose the weakness of human lives, there is nothing that can stop him. And he knows how to choose his time.

It has been demonstrated that "both in conception and practice the visionary qualities of Soyinka's art have striking affinities with the tradition of European Romanticism." Soyinka adapts mythic patterns, persons and values drawn from the traditional wisdom, infusing them as he does so with the urgency of his conviction of their relevance to a world which, like that of the early nineteenth century, is marked by continuous political, industrial and social revolution and disorder." He believes that "this inherited wisdom reveals truths which his contemporaries ignore only at their greatest peril." He thinks that "this myth of Ogun's quest across the gulf of transition as a revelation of the necessity for the contemporary psyche to enter into restorative mystical communion with its cosmic environment" is profoundly significant. Soyinka's romantic idealism is revealed in the three plays *A Dance of the Forests, The Strong Breed* (1964) and *The Road*. These plays assert "the Romantic belief in the need for individual self-discovery in the face of conventional values" of tradition. Soyinka seems to suggest that the artist's voice of vision is found through exile and arduous re-discovery and re-formulation of the ancient values of tradition, but not through the unquestioning acceptance of inherited truths. "This idea is embodied in the artist Demoke in *A Dance of the Forests*. The "redemptive sacrifice" of Demoke has the "symbolic reference to the history of the peoples of Nigeria and indeed of the African continent over many centuries. Demoke succeeds in his revolt against the perennial cycle of human stupidity and brutality where Eshuoro and the dead Warrior have failed." In the play "the living want the Gathering of the Tribes to be a glorification of past history, and they are angry when their guests from the ancestor world turn out to be reminders of the inheritance of brutality and evil." A truly modern human state, Soyinka seems to suggest, will emerge from the unity of past, present and future in the moment of vision. The tradition is revitalized "through visionary self-discovery and regeneration." In other words, "the inheritance of traditional wisdom," Soyinka believes, should be directed to "a humanistic re-formulation" which is facilitated by the "visionary quest" of "a heroically personal experience of self-discovery and self-renewal." Such an approach to the elucidation of Soyinka's plays is a considerable help to the readers as Soyinka is a "difficult" writer "even for those who share his cultural background."

Eunuchs of Will: Power and Power Mongers: Wole Soyinka's *The Road* and *Death and the King's Horseman*

M. PUSHPA

We do not burn the woods to trap
A squirrel; we do not ask the mountain's
Aid, to crack a walnut.

Soyinka

Life is a circular journey back to the primal home. This journey is a potent figure for the long, hard struggle of the mind to achieve an imaginative liberation which will serve as a restorative. Self-division and self-conflict are two obstacles which can be removed if we overcome the psychic antagonists. We should be able to see the glory of man's original oneness with nature. Creative art is a product of and the medium for the imagination's struggle towards a liberated self-awareness. Coleridge provided an effective emblem for imagination in depicting it as a serpent with its tail in its mouth, forever flowing into itself, without beginning or end. Myth-making becomes an essential part of any artist's creativity. Soyinka depicted gods as descending to the earth to be reunited with human essence. The first one to bridge the gulf of separation was the leader of the gods, Ogun, with his power of the will. Ogun becomes the embodiment of the creative will and its manifestations in human knowledge. The metaphysical concepts of Soyinka and the Romantics are built on the myth of a primal severance of human essence from cosmic oneness. This abyss can be bridged only by an immense will, and it involves the disintegration of the quester's self in order to bridge the gulf with visionary hopes. This pilgrimage is an arduous one. The undertaking sometimes destroys the person as the self is severed from all social anchorage. He becomes a restless soul, endowed with desperate energy in search of a lost vision. This is relevant to the pilgrimage undertaken by the poet. With Soyinka's heroes, the situation is more or less the same. Men who follow in the footsteps of the successful Ogun may suffer disintegration of their individual selfhoods. Ogun is "the paradoxical truth of destructiveness and creativeness in acting man" (*Myth* 150). He is the artistic spirit and the first tragic actor. The protagonist of the Yoruba 'ritual of archetypes' is a surrogate for Ogun and his experience of ritual possession is actually reliving of the god's dissolution and reintegration. "The actor in the ritual drama . . . prepares mentally and physically for his disintegration and re-assembly within the universal womb of origin, experiences the transitional, yet inchoate matrix of death and being" (*Myth* 30). There is a mingling of experiences in this typical Nigerian setting. A specific ethnic situation calls for ritual celebration. In *The Road*, such a situation is delineated. Each evening, the Professor serves palm-wine in a version of the communion rite which complements the service held in the Church.

Myth is a story or a narrative; it is a blaze of reality. 'Collective unconscious' is universal—it contains contents and ways of behaviour which are more or less the same everywhere. Jung pays "lip-service to the universality of a collective unconscious, and to the archetype as the inhabitant of that hinterland" (*Myth* 35). From this, we get myths which are psychic phenomena. The primitive man has the tendency to assimilate all our outer sense experiences, and they coalesce with the inner psychic events. We are always in the centre of actions which we perform, but cannot control. The tragedy is that mankind is powerless against mankind, and the gods show it in the ways of fate. We are our masters in the realm of consciousness. Once we step out of its shadow we discover that there are certain unseen forces operating on us. The sense of our inadequacy leaves us a little startled. A state of panic is created as our closely guarded supremacy of consciousness is questioned. We find ourselves on the slippery foothold of insecurity. We need moral courage to ask the right question, but we lack it. The unpredictable behaviour of our psyche is another threat to our consciousness. The inner forces always pose a threat, much more than the external forces. Our unconscious is one stretch of water which hides the treasure in its depths. Our ideas struggle to come to the surface. The struggle becomes more titanic as the pressure from outside forces mounts on the ideas. The question of man's spirituality comes up. We take recourse to myths, customs and rituals to express our pent-up feelings. Here, too, there is a problem. A stray individual with a strong will puts up a stiff fight against these rituals, as he starts questioning their very validity.

The inner world is described as the "primal reality, the hinterland of transition" (*Myth* 33). Myth was created out of ritual. The latter term must be understood in a wide sense, because in primitive society everything is sacred, nothing profane. Every action—eating, drinking, telling, fighting—has its proper place and is holy. The rituals help in the cathartic process of the individuals. The ritual process reflects the archetypal struggle of the moral being against external forces.

It is not impertinent on our part to regard the importance of myths in the study of Soyinka's plays. He has gone on record regarding this point. He has declared that myth, especially the myth of Ogun, is a good means of channelising the power of the people into constructive courses and that study of myths gives us valuable insights into society. The Yoruba pantheon of gods is a large one consisting of nearly four hundred gods. The Supreme god is called Olorun. His name could mean "the Owner of Heaven." He is omnipotent and possesses wisdom. He is immortal and has the power to judge. Ogun is another important god, the god of iron and steel. Originally, he was a hunter deity. When gods descended to the earth, the *terra firma*, Ogun at first preferred to live on high mountains. Later, he returned to social life. He is the one who prepared the road through the thicket for other deities. He is the god of war, hunting, blacksmiths, engineers, mechanics, lorry drivers, barbers, butchers, and carvers. He is by nature hard and fierce, but is not evil. He demands justice, free play and rectitude.

Ogun was the god who made the heroic attempt to reunite the gods and men. He has revitalised the spiritual life of the gods and men. He represents the pioneering spirit and the urge to challenge the revolutionary principle. The "men of Ogun" who appear in Soyinka's plays have a burning desire for revitalising the existing order of things. They pose a challenge to the society which they want to revamp. We do not fully comprehend the first outcome of their heroic challenges. Daodu in *Kongi's Harvest* is forced to run away from his country. Olunde in *Death and the King's Horseman* commits the ritual suicide in his father's stead. In either of these cases, we are not informed of the final consequences of their actions. These men in Soyinka's plays are not supermen. They do not offer any definite solutions to the social, historical and metaphysical problems they wrestle with. They pave the way for positive solutions. What we gather from Soyinka's plays is that we can find solutions for the problems dealt with. To obtain this one needs as a prerequisite the presence of strong, self-dependent, tenacious individuals who dare "clear a path" for the timid ones. There are people who have the desire, but lack the spirit of enterprise, the will. These "men of

Ogun" have this power which serves as a beacon-light for the less enterprising ones. Ogun and his representatives stand for positive attitude to life—for optimism.

Ogun and other gods had to drink at the fount of mortality as they wanted to inspect humanity. A long period of isolation had created a wide chasm, and Ogun finally decided to take the plunge. He however refused to accept the crown offered by the people. At first, he presented himself in a frightening attire, which repelled people. Later, he came down decked in palm fronds and was crowned king. A barrel of wine attracted Ogun and in his intoxicated state he indulged in slaughtering his men-friends and foes alike. Yet he did not forbid the use of palm-wine in his worship. As Soyinka says, "Ogun is the embodiment of challenge, the Promethean instinct in man, constantly at the service of society for its self-realisation" (*Myth* 30). Ogun thus becomes the embodiment of the social, communal will invested in a protagonist of his choice. Soyinka himself could be one, and he in turn creates heroes in his plays, embodying this will.

Yoruba concept of morality is that which creates harmony in the cosmos. According to Soyinka, dream images and psychotic exhalation are not in the category of archetypes. These are mere emanations from the ephemeral and transient portions of the human psyche. Archetypes, on the other hand, proceed from the congealed substrata of the psyche, which are constantly enriched by the moral and historic experience of man. Morality in Yoruba world view is linked with the mandatory compensations that nature demands.

Soyinka justified his addiction to myth and ritual as both of them are relevant to the spiritual needs of modern man. The story and myth are interrelated, just as society and the individual are interrelated. Soyinka is a Yoruba writer, but how much he was addicted to the Yoruba myth is a matter of conjecture. All that he likes is to retell the myths, not as a theologian but for the benefit of culturally-deprived English scholars. With the Yoruba myth to help him, Soyinka has his one foot planted in the eternal, and the other in the present. In *Idanre*, he uses the electricity playing along a high-tension wire in a storm as the fusion of Sango and Ogun, whom he identifies as the "gods of lightning and electricity." Soyinka's plays deal with the destruction of men by men or by forces which they cannot propitiate. Ogun stands for humane but rigidly restorative justice. His use of myths does not restrict his universality.

Ogun's action is a drama of individual stress. The protagonist is mentally and physically prepared for his disintegration. The tragic action in Yoruba drama stems from a knowledge of the re-charged energies. The Yoruba metaphysical world is characterised by a gulf which has to be constantly diminished by sacrifices, rituals, ceremonies of appeasement to the cosmic powers which guard the gulf. Ogun seems to incorporate all these qualities in him. *The Road* and *Death and the King's Horseman* are plays which focus their attention on this metaphysical world. *The Road* was performed in 1965 in London. The scene of action is a motor road somewhere in Nigeria. Professor, who is the protagonist of the play, owns a shop where he sells the parts of wrecked cars to drivers who are in need of them. There are other persons around Professor who depend on the road for their livelihood. There is Kotonu, an erstwhile lorry-driver who now assists Professor in his business. Samson, Kotonu's companion, and tout, is distressed with Kotonu's indifference to his profession. There is Salubi, a private chauffeur, who has managed to obtain a driver's uniform, but has no driving licence. Say Tokyo Kid is a typical character, very relevant to the universal political scene. He is a lorry driver, but is more interested in leading a gang of hooligans. This gang helps politicians in disrupting meetings of the opponents. Particulars Joe is another typical character—a corrupt policeman, who fits into the scene smoothly. Professor himself was a Sunday-school teacher and a lay preacher in a church close to his shop. He lost his position in the church after charges of embezzlement of funds and drunken misbehaviour were foisted on him. Professor lost his faith in the validity of Christian teaching, but retained his interest in spiritual matters. He is obsessed with one idea—to find the key to the mysterious truth which he calls "the word," and which he believes is closely related to Death. He firmly believes that we cannot understand the meaning of life, unless we understand the meaning of death. This notion prompts him to settle close to the road, as a number of accidents occur there. He even manipulates certain accidents especially when he runs short of spare parts in his shop. He has a lucrative business.

Professor and his parishioners conduct a kind of communion, different from that being administered in the church. They drink palm-wine served by Murano. Murano is taking part in a religious feast in honour of Ogun. He is possessed by God, and runs across the road. He is run over by Kotonu, who is driving the lorry, and could not apply the brakes on time. Professor is happy to keep Murano with him, as he feels that Murano is close to death. He is keen on his doing the ritual dance, so that he could get a revelation of the Word. Say Tokyo Kid makes an attempt to stop the ritual dance, and in the fight that ensues both Professor and Say Tokyo Kid are killed.

The tragic grandeur of the play is balanced by a pettiness and a low-level corruption in the means whereby he tries to achieve his ends. The play is about a search for hidden knowledge in a world of broken traditions and cultural chaos. It is represented in the form of a quest by a man for the essence of death. The scenario is very bleak, and is marked with despondency. Established religion has become a distant memory unable to maintain its hold over people's mind. There is a spiritual vacuum and the individual quester is left alone to seek his salvation. Professor, once a Christian, is a lonely pathfinder. Underneath this frenzied search, there is a process at work, symbolised by Ogun. This is the law which says that man will destroy man by his relentless search for progress. Here, individual will dominates by its pride and arrogance and by massive self-centredness which is a denial of the common interest. Professor is one such representation. His mysterious words cast a spell on everyone. His quest is awe-inspiring, as he is keen on finding out the meaning of death. Professor hardly deserves our admiration as he is a crook, an expert in forgery and a thief. He engineers road deaths, by manipulating the road signs. He sends others to the boundary between life and death in his search for knowledge. Through the strange vision he possesses, we are able to see the deeply embedded need in man for possession of ultimate knowledge and power. How he plans to fulfil his ambitions forms the crux of the play.

Word is the moving force in the play. Professor is looking out for the Word—he is partly mad, partly inspired. He is as enigmatic as the Word. He ceaselessly attempts to define the elusive Word. He seeks the help of Christian imagery. "There are dangers in the Quest I know, but the Word may be found companion not to life, but Death. Three souls you know, fled up that tree. . . . They died, all three of them crucified on rigid branches" (159). His quest leads him into a state of frenzied activity. He can see nothing else but the Word. "I am so confused, but I have sight and vision only for the Word, and it may chance, sometimes that I miss my way among worldly humans" (158). Though Professor is always in the proximity of death, he is not able to get to the depth of its meaning. He has not been able to get close to a dying person in order to find out what one sees and hears at the moment of one's passage. He is happy to find Murano in a semi-dying state. He hopes to get the revelation of the Word, and pass it on to his disciples. He has the ability to penetrate sensitively into another world.

Appearances are deceptive, and so it is with Professor. He appears to be a bundle of contradictions, but he is not. He is a perfect deceiver—as a seeker and as a forger of driver's licences. As a seeker he is deceiving others, as well as himself. The Word is enshrouded in a haze which cannot be penetrated. Murano is the only crutch on which Professor leans for his spiritual aid, but Murano has been deprived of the power of speech. Professor claims that Murano is the sole guardian of the Word. People like him in a state of suspension of death "have slept beyond the portals of secrets. They have pierced the guard of eternity and unearthed the Word, a golden nugget on the tongue. And so their tongue hangs heavy and they are forever silenced" (186). Professor contemplates on a piece of paper, which deceives him. The piece of paper turns out to be a completed football pools coupon. "Oh God, Oh God, the enormity of unknown burdens, of hidden wisdoms . . . say the Word in our time O Lord, utter the hidden Word" (203). The high-expectancy atmosphere is deflated by his companion's answer that they are football pools coupons.

The Aksident store is a money-spinning proposition. Professor sells parts of wrecked cars. He 'sells' his advice at exorbitant prices. Manipulation is an art he has perfected, and does not mind practising it on his disciples, if it brings him close to truth. To cheat is his motto, and he has no qualms about it. His goal is absolute knowledge, but he is not prepared to make personal sacrifices. He believes that he can make use of Ogun, whose spirit dwells in Murano's body. "I must hope, even now. I cannot yet believe that death's revelation must be total, or not at all" (226). He has failed to realise that absolute knowledge cannot be achieved if one is firmly anchored in the world of living. Whoever wants to gain insight into the mysteries of being, of existence, must die—either ritually, like Murano, or physically like Professor. He realises the truth, while on the threshold of death. "Breathe like the road, be even like the road itself" (228). Whoever thinks that he can arrive at the truth using the path of intellect is actually on the wrong track.

The road symbolizes Ogun. The overall impression of Professor's last words is that they are obscure. The monologue ends abruptly, as death intervenes. We wonder if he is exhorting us to prey upon one another: an exhortation to the seeker of truth to accept death as something natural. Professor's "intellectual grope" ends with his death.

Ogun dominates the play with his presence. He is the road and is in possession of the Truth. Anyone who wants to get at the Truth must surrender himself to Ogun, even at the risk of his life. Ogun wants to accept death as a prelude to life; from the decay of the dead past comes new life. Ogun is not in favour of death as a result of political violence, or of sheer carelessness. Ritual death results in temporary effacement of individual personality, and is attainable in the ecstasy of ritual dancing. A meaningful life is one in which we have realized the absolute oneness of everything that exists. Professor gets this realization through the agency of Ogun, for he is stabbed with a knife, an instrument made of steel, which is sacred to Ogun. It is Ogun, in the guise of the possessed Murano, who slays the champion of meaningless killing, Say Tokyo Kid.

Ritual drama has its roots in the community festival, like a re-enactment of historical events. The actors may lose their personalities by impersonating others. One of the Yoruba travelling theatres which emerged from a society of masqueraders, is known as *egungun*. The function of this society was to worship and appease the dead ancestors. These ritual plays are performed in front of the royal palace in an open space, by members of the ruling family, which has selected the Oba, a king. Their subjects are taken from mythology—creation of the world, of gods, the lives of ancestors, and their mutual relationship. The masks worn are the impersonations of ancestors.

Murano is possessed by a god. As Soyinka remarks in his prefatory note, he functions as "an arrest of time, or death" (149). In a ritual dance, the actor is in constant fear of his personality merging with the character he is impersonating. It is this aspect which terrified Kotonu. The mask of Agemo hovers in the background throughout the play. Murano is trapped in the moment when he is experiencing the transition. The Word is the guiding force of Professor's life, and the motive for his quest. It summons up the traditional divine power of God's word, which was the medium of his communion with men. It is related to the divine pattern of which our world is a copy. Christ becomes the Word. Professor assimilates all these meanings and strives to add on the secret knowledge of the transition between life and death.

The Yoruba cult has its parallel practices in the Christian tradition. Professor appears to be both the leader of a Christian and a traditional cult. His daily ritual evening communion synchronises with the communion within the church; the distribution of palm wine parallels the distribution of communion wine and his final speech is uttered by the gesture of a hand, 'like a benediction.' The features of the traditional African cult are found here—a temple (the Aksident store), a priest, whose duty is to keep the community in touch with the ancestors (Professor), sacrifice (here deaths on the road), possession by the spirits of the dead ancestors (the egungun maskers). Like a priest and a cult leader, Professor wears a specific dress (a Victorian-style suit and a monocle). He is endowed with psychic ability to divine secret meanings; with his special skill of divination, he interprets printed texts and signs. Though aware of his failure to discover the Word, he is overwhelmed by a sense of its nearness. This failure finds its outlet in frequent outbursts of temper: "Take your snail slime secreted eyes off the living testament before I poke them off. Do you think I would foul up eternal beads of cowries with muted commerce?" (201). He leans heavily on Murano for the Word.

The Aksident Store is furnished with spare parts garnered from road accidents. In his shack, a slice of Nigerian subculture—the atmosphere, idiom, hopes and aspirations—of the "motor park" is dramatized. People of all sorts haunt this place—drivers and their touts, unemployed men, thugs, political opportunists who supplement their incomes by taking part in profitable political conflicts. These 'layabouts' occupy a 'sort of island of lost souls' presided over by Professor whose own soul is not lost, but is of another order. The characters assembled in the shack belong to the lower classes. One of them is Kotonu, a competent driver, who has given up the road after two near-escapes from death. He is Professor's new business partner—'keeping shop for the mortuary'—as Samson puts it disgustingly. He is mentally shaken and despite warnings from his friends, he goes to the scene of accident. Professor describes the accident as "showers of crystals flying on broken souls" (159). The accidents are signposts on the road of his quest for Word, which is the essence of Death itself. Professor tries every channel to find out the meaning of Death, but fails. As a last resort, he tries to investigate death through Ogun mask, and forces Murano to wear the mask. Face to face with the Egungun, the spirit of death, Professor hopes to understand this ultimate event. The people gathered around are struck with terror at Professor's trivializing the ritual. "Do you want to go blind from things you shouldn't see?" remarks Say Tokyo Kid (227). He prevails on him to stop it, but Professor is adamant in his refusal to abandon this ritual. Professor approaches a spiritual issue like death analytically. He has a sense of contempt for the lower classes. "If you think I do this [providing shelter for the unemployed] from the kindness of my heart you are fools" (221). He uses all his intellectual resources in order to make money. He charges the illiterate exorbitant "consultation fees" even when they want to discuss a simple problem. Forging drivers' licences is an artistic endeavour for him. He feels that his powers are on the wane and that life is receding from him. This needs a little adjustment. He justifies his illegal activity as "a solution, a compensation, a redress, a balance of inequalities" (187). and ignores its fatal ramifications.

Soyinka seems sceptical of the cost of progress and brings out the paradoxical nature of progress. The central symbol of the road embodies the educational progress or technological advancement. Before Nigeria obtained its independence, the colonial rulers had constructed roads across the country for exploiting natural resources. The bureaucratic set-up encouraged corruption among petty officials and semi-literate individuals like Professor who have found a niche for their parasitical activities. The very modernism which has given a face-lift to Nigerian social and economic life has also endowed the westernised class with ways of exploiting their own lower classes. Professor is a representative of this exploiting class. It is pertinent to note here that this kind of situation is universal, not one peculiar to Nigerian political or social scenario.

The road is fraught with dangers, as it is infested with reckless drivers. There is an air of uncertainty about one reaching the destination—it is very similar to the lack of direction which characterised Nigerian society in 1965. The road is used as a symbol to capture the transitional stage of his country and its very precarious socio-political state on the verge of civil war. He was appalled by the large number of road fatalities on Nigerian highways. Kotonu remarks, "The road and the spider is gloating. Then the fly buzzes along like a happy fool" (178). In one of his poems, "In Memory of Segun Awolowo," Soyinka characterises the road as "the aged road/retched on this fresh plunder/of my youth" (*Idanre and Other Poems* 14).

Professor is the type of westernised Yoruba, who is caught between two worlds. Christianity has failed him, and he is alienated from his traditional religion. He attempts to adopt his powers of ratiocination to solve a spiritual problem. The traditionalist, perhaps, has found a way of ritually containing the fearful reality of death, whereas Professor, has not been able to do so.

The wall in the church comes down. This symbolises the collapse of the false edifice they had set up. The community had pursued the shadow of Christian practice. The collapse of the wall symbolises the triumph of external forces over the church. One significant observation is that there is no difference in the standard of morality between the church community and the one outside it. Professor was in the forefront of the Christian onslaught, and was involved in the embezzlement of Church funds. He and others interpreted the Christian injunction in a narrow way. After leaving the church, he becomes wiser. He feels that the Word cannot be found in the church where there is so much hypocrisy. His search for the Word develops into necromantic practice.

The role played by rituals is significant. The play is built around the Yoruba cult of 'agemo.' Soyinka himself explains: "Agemo is simply a religious cult of flesh dissolution. . . . Agemo, the mere phase includes the passage of transition from the human to the divine essence" (149). Murano functions as an arrest of time, or death, since he was knocked down by a lorry in his "agemo" stage. Soyinka uses 'agemo' the sense of illusion in the egungun masquerade but there is no attempt at illusion. The metaphysical aspect of 'agemo' is what impresses the dramatist—"flesh dissolution." The idea of the searcher after the meaning of death, who has to die is "very Yoruba." Professor has the Yoruba idea that death reveals itself to humans only in their own death. The road is a hungry, man-devouring monster. Professor urges the travellers to be aggressors—they can achieve this by imbibing the very qualities of the road—a snake-like deceit and treachery. In essence, his quest fails since, according to Soyinka, both religious structures—the church and the traditional Yoruba religion—turn out to be "restricted by orthodox acceptances." Soyinka describes Professor as a "Charlatan, outcast, yet communal, teacher and quester, innocent and cunning, a stray among strays, priest and profaner, moulder and iconoclast, the community [traditional Yoruba believers] which he, in effect, appropriates and opposes to the one which cast him out proves, in the end, just as controlled and restricted by orthodox acceptances as the former" (qtd. in Katrak 74).

The theme of death is well analysed in *The Road*—death as 'gruesome' reality as well as a trade. One is aware of proximity to death. The spider's web in a corner, and the alert spider is itself an eloquent symbol of the theme. The game of death is played by Ogun, who reveals in unseasonal harvests, such as the death of the playwright's friend, Segun Awolowo. It was "plunder of my youth," he says. Death has been the "scrap-iron dealer." The paradox in Soyinka's concept of tragedy is the contradiction between Ogun's caprice and man's Free Will. This imparts a touch of irony. The road could be the proverbial road of life, along which men must travel. It could also be a symbol of progress, a notion ridiculed by Soyinka in many of his works, who would question the

Wrathful wings of Man's Progression . . .
But such another Wraith! Brother,
Silenced in the startled hug of
Your invention—is the mocked grimace
This closed contortion—I?
("Death in the Dawn," *Idanre and Other Poems*)

The lorry drivers are Ogun's devotees—their masquerade is in his honour. Most of the characters in *The Road* are groping in the twilight zone. Soyinka chooses a sort of no-man's land—belonging neither to the world of flesh nor the spirit. Hence, the significance of 'agemo' is a visual suspension of death.

This movement of transition—dark, middle area—suggests the overall position of Africa caught in the middle way. Professor is a sort of amphibian creature, neither African nor European. The cultural clash is represented by him. The modern African is nagged by psychological problems. Professor shows signs of lunacy or schizophrenia. He becomes a symbol of Africa's unique position. Africa follows absurdly the fashion of Europe at a distance, and never catches up. He is between the two worlds—his connection with Christianity and his closeness to the worshippers of Ogun. Besides Professor, there are men with names inspired by American crime and Western films, like Say Tokyo Kid. Such people adopt a Chicago gangster's drawl, yet sing traditional Yoruba praise songs and worship Ogun. "Say Tokyo Kid represents an ugly fusion of the traditionally African and the hard-headed materialism of an alien culture" (Roscoe 230). Murano represents the unadulterated old order. He is a palm-wine tapper, the representative of a traditional rural occupation. He has no ability to talk or to hear—he is dead and is sinking towards dissolution.

The play is an eloquent comment on Nigerian society. It is, in fact, a bitter attack. The whole society reeks with the stench of disintegration and death. There is no character in the play who is not diseased—there is an ambience of vice and greed. The play presents a grim picture of gloom and decadence, where a dog-eat-dog morality rules supreme. People like Sergeant Burma and Professor are ruthless and indifferent to human loss. Kotonu makes this remark about Professor: "He was moving around those corpses as if they didn't exist. All he cared about was re-planting that sign-post. To see him you would think he was Adam re-planting the Tree of Life" (167). Advocates of peace and non-violence would be appalled at the alarming conditions of the Nigerian society.

where the common people are preying on one another like hyenas. Corruption pervades every aspect of life—law, religion, human relations. The play is like Soyinka's writing on the nation's wall. He depicts a society which has lost its grip over the essentials of life, and is on the road to dissolution and death; perhaps, death is a prelude to rebirth. The theme is tragedy of human waste and loss of life. The playwright described it "as based on . . . a personal intimacy with a certain aspect of the road. . . . It concerns, he said, a search into the essence of death" (Gibbs 78). Professor is desirous of penetrating the very heart of phenomena. He seeks a categorical certainty, which is alien to a Yoruba world-view, a world-view rooted in "the very indeterminacy of Truth" (Gibbs 78).

Professor is a typical Westernised Yoruba caught between two worlds. Christianity has not given him the strength he needed, and he is alienated from his traditional religion. He is an individualist, and worse than that, he is eccentric. We agree with Katrak when she says that "Professor's abuse of his literacy and education is symptomatic of the paradoxical nature of progress" (64). The network of roads is symbolic of the bureaucratic system of regulations, licences and taxes. This set-up has encouraged corruption.

Two focal points are provided in the play—Professor and Kotonu. Professor has a colonial background. As a young man he had waged holy war against palm-wine bars; later, he became lay-reader and then left the church. A complex character like Professor can never be defined—part wise man and part fool. Kotonu is a driver by profession. He would not run over dogs as other drivers did as a ritual of sacrifice for Ogun, in the belief that Ogun accepts the dogs as sacrifices and protects the interests of the drivers. Kotonu is haunted by a guilty conscience as he knocked down an *egungun* figure, Murano, who was taking part in a drivers' festival. Kotonu, stunned by this tragic event, withdrew into himself, bewildered, unable to understand any thing that had happened to him.

The protagonist in the ritual drama is entrusted with the task of uniting the "essence-ideal" with "materiality." The ritual is a cleansing—a kind of recreative ceremony aimed at diminishing the gulf of transition, and, thus strengthening the psyche of the community. Yoruba culture retained the collective experience as a living reality. Professor is a character who defies analysis. A charismatic character, he defeats our efforts at identifying him as a specific type. He is verbose, though uneducated, eccentric, and is intoxicated with the 'learning.' His quest is the vicarious experience of the passage from life to death in the belief that "the Word may be found companion not to life but to Death" (159). He is doubtful whether the Word exists in the church. "I stood often behind the bronze wings of the eagle; on the broad span of the eagle's outstretched wings rested the Word—oh what a blasphemy it all was but I did not know it" (205). His haunts are next to the shadows of death. The quest leads him from the respectable brass lectern to the driver's shack, but it can only be found in death.

The Road is a 'problem' play, in the sense that it suffers from obscurity of meaning. In a review, a critic seems to hold an unintentional scare for the reader in its ironic title: "Keep off the Road." One does find a vintage Soyinka in the play. The subject of death by road appeared earlier in his poem "Death in the Dawn," and the Segun Awolowo poem. In "Death in the Dawn," dawn is a time of hope, tinted with fear. The people make their way to the market in the early morning mist. The men have not found the meaning of life; they are groping in the dark. The road waits for them and devours them. Soyinka captures the sudden transformation from life to death which takes place when the car crashes. Man is trapped in his own invention. Progress has only exposed man to more frightening forms of death. In "In Memory of Segun Awolowo" the grief is personal. Death is not mere abstraction for him, but a concrete foe. His triumph is certain, but what makes it revolting is that our fellow-men are in league with Death. Professor is keen on finding out the meaning of Death, though it is very elusive. These poems together show satirical and spiritual attitudes in the play. The road links the two attitudes of the play by being the agent of death, as well as the path along which the dead passengers are carried to their dumb funeral.

Professor's quest is not merely intellectual—it has emotional as well as personal overtones. He is groping his way through the evening of life towards death, and also the achievement of that divine status, which he lost by his fall from ecclesiastical grace. He is nagged by the feeling of guilt over the embezzlement of church funds. He appears to be a mad man to some people because of his verbal virtuosity. He cannot define the Word, but he uses it in changing and bewildering context. The Word becomes an elusive landmark which Professor fails to lay his hands on. He insists on saying that the Word is growing, and its growth is determined by the context in which it is placed. His attempt at replanting the tree of life represents his own transplant. It is a symbolic need for his new shack community to which he has been driven as replacement for the Christian community from which he has been uprooted. Death is described as a harvest, and the meanings gained at the scene of an accident are the offerings of the hungry god. He believes that road deaths will lead him to the Word. The Word may be found "where ascent is broken, and a winged secret plummets back to earth" (157).

The quest for the Word goes beyond the desire for knowledge to a longing for self-deification. The Word is elusive, trapped in the "slumbering chrysalis of the Word" (157). Professor's search for it among the rejects, abandoned scraps of paper, newspaper and the like, indicates a topsy-turvydom in which the hierarchical values are reversed. This reversal of values is seen in Professor's association of the Word with Death. Such an association is in contrast with the fundamental Christian belief, according to which Christ is seen as the Saviour, who shows the way, to the Truth and the Life throughout Eternity. It is also in conflict with the Yoruba teaching which recognizes the duality of life-and-death forces. Professor's assumptions are at odds with established religious beliefs, whether Christian or Yoruba "he flutters mid-way between the practices of the church, and the beliefs of Yoruba religion and culture" (Peters 191).

We participate with Professor in his quest. We realise that faith in a number of institutions has been shaken, but the faith is not yet destroyed. This key to human life is beyond our grasp. "In the course of the play, the pace of transition is quickened and the community is driven to an important, crucial road junction. . . . As Professor, the shepherd of that inglorious flock dies we find we are at the end of an era" (Ogunba 147).

Soyinka is concerned with the spiritual quest. An artist is the voice of vision in his own time. His mythmaking revolves around the imperative need for a spiritual life and art which has links with the past and is a transformation of it. He reformulates with the help of a heroically personal experience of self-discovery and self-renewal, and the path of visionary quest. The whole play assumes the form of a myth or a symbol. Professor represents the perennial instinct in man, which yearns to explain the complex world he lives in. Man tries to probe the foundation of his existence, and to discover a meaning for life. This effort leads him beyond the physical forces, to gods and spirits. Physical forces alone do not explain the value of human existence. Kotonu reflects on his and Samson's narrow escape from death. The people in the lorry which overtook them on the bridge are killed while they are spared. Hence, Professor is determined to investigate the nature of death and understand its secret. This understanding could lead to an extension of life's meaning through an extension of mortality into immortality.

The dance of possession is the climax of the action in *The Road.* The dance represents the blending of the religious elements in traditional culture and Christian doctrine, as well as the violence found in the technological society. The dance is a desperate bid to unearth the secret of death; a secret beyond the limits of man's knowledge. The widely held belief was that a god becomes manifest during the transitional dance of possession. These principles coalesce within the framework of the road. The road is a preserve of Ogun, and is a symbol of the process of technology in the development and the use of machine—in the impact of technology on the environment, and in the violent destruction of lives through accidents.

The road is not a fixed symbol—it is a path as well as a predator. As a path it is the physical road that we tread. It is also a trajectory of Professor's quest and a medium of benefits and scourges of civilisation. The road's rapacious nature matches the spider's function as a similarly vicious predator trapping victims in its artistic web of destruction. Professor is not a representative quester charting out a path for everyman to follow. He has rejected the accepted beliefs as illusion of the Word. He decides to achieve the positive through the negative; to find life through death, value through rejection. He exploits the castaways and wants their lives to end in meaningless death. He does not hide his regret that no one has died in the motor accident. He rushes to the site of the accident to arrest the flight of the souls of the newly dead in order to pluck from them the secret of death and life. He plucks the cautionary road sign and plants the sign 'bend.' All this is part of the intellectual striving after the Word, as essence of death. It is self-pride which propels Professor to know what only the Gods know. Man's egoism has led him to believe that he cannot be confined to earthly life like other creatures. Professor's egoism displays his extraordinary insolence, the insolence of a man with a will to power and knowledge.

Professor is a composite of earlier protagonists, Brother Jero and Eman. Jero's longing for sainthood is surpassed by Professor's yearning for knowledge and godhead in *The Road.* Eman's death like Professor's fails to confirm our belief in the value of human life. Professor's inordinate desire for the power of knowledge is not as devastating as the savage propensities of Kongi and Dr. Bero, who have modern weapons of war at their disposal. Professor feels that he has the capacity to combat the consequences of sacrilege as he has superior understanding. Professor is a cross between a quack and a mad man—he is a maverick.

The Road is a satirical attack on the official order of things. Soyinka ridicules the whole official order that mindlessly repeats the errors of established authority. The countryside of Western Nigeria is cut by creeks and streams, some of them with deep channels and the highways include curves and bridges which are likely to be damaged due to rains. The major accident in the play takes place on a "rotten bridge." It is the result of apparently insane officiousness.

II

The norms of social behaviour bind together the various individuals in a society. Selfishness and egoism could be the prime movers for an individual to take a bold step. It could be, sometimes, the genuine interest in revamping the social set-up. Nevertheless, it is the individual will which prompts men to be creative. The conflict between will and demands of the society forms the crux of many plays. *Death and the King's Horseman* (1975) is one such play. It is based on the events in Yorubaland during the 1960s, when an English District Commissioner tried to prevent an Oba from performing a ritualistic suicide which had been demanded of the chief's horseman by tradition. The son feels humiliated by his father's act and commits suicide; the father follows suit in the presence of the District officer. Soyinka does not adhere to historical accuracy. The background is the Second World War and the English Prince visits the place. The horseman's son is educated in the West. All this helps to create parallels and contrasts between European and Yoruba concepts of personal honour, of self-sacrifice for communal welfare and of the need to face death.

The central concern in Yoruba society is the preservation of the community. Soyinka affirms the dying tradition of ritualistic self-sacrifice, because it forms the crux of his vision, which is based on African sense of communal well-being. There is a continuity between the living and the dead, the human and the divine, man and nature, sky and earth. If the horseman fails to perform his duty as sacrificial messenger to the gods, the community is put at risk. The play's focus is on the cultural conflict, as well as the horseman's weakness when he is faced by death. He is reluctant to leave the pleasures of life. If he does not die, and if his son dies first then the cycle of life of seasonal harvest is ruptured. Through a poetic vision of images, symbols, and allusions, Soyinka depicts this tragedy. To the Englishman it is just clash of cultures, but the symbols of Yoruba myths mean much more. The infusion of the old and the new is like lightning because it is god Sango's lightning entering the receiving earth. The horseman suffers from a lack of will. The psychological struggle of the main character becomes the centre of action. He is fettered from within—he wonders if the gods have marked him out to be destroyer of society as a result of his dereliction of duty. "Death as an act of will, affirms his identity and destiny" (King 344).

Any country, any 'world' has its roots in its myths, mores and history. The African world, too, exists on such an infrastructure. It also possesses the virtues of complementarity and 'common humanity.' An impressionistic insight into customs and social structure is inextricably woven into the fabric of the play. Elesin finds the world to be good, and it is his duty to keep it so. The world is like a hive or an ant-hill—none of them can wander, it has its roots. The mystery of life is deep and one has to be immersed in it. We cannot see.

> The still great womb of the world—
> No man beholds his mother's womb—
> Yet who denies it's there? Coiled
> To the navel of the world is that
> Endless cord that links us all. (157)

If we are to lose our way, this trailing cord will bring us back to the roots. One cannot miss the emphasis on the debt to the community. We are a part of the society. A strong will is needed to break this entanglement. How far one will achieve success, depends on the circumstances in which he is placed.

A white character is used to define Yoruba values. Jane Pilkings considers the act of the horseman killing himself as a barbaric act. It is feudal—the king dies and along with him the chieftain is burned. The westerners have the knack of giving refined names. War is a kind of suicide, and Olunde sees nothing amoral in the ritual suicide. The realities of war are more brutal and inhuman than this, and the whites indulge in this worst type of brutality. A disaster beyond human reckoning is passed off as a triumph. The native's mental landscape is not altered by the Western education—he remains firmly rooted in the subsoil of tradition. Olunde has given up his father as dead even when the king was declared dead, as the ritual demanded the horseman's death. Olunde may be branded a 'savage,' or an 'impudent nigger' as he never doubts the necessity of sacrificial custom. A hereditary officer, the king's horseman must die within thirty days of the King's death. This ritual suicide is enacted by a powerful act of the individual's will-power, and without any external stimulus. The whiteman, Pilkings, prevents Elesin from committing suicide. Soyinka keeps the colonial factor only as a catalytic incident.

Olunde's insistence on the ritual suicide is not a celebration of the Yoruba ritual. Soyinka ia not writing a polemic aimed at practical re-introduction of ritual suicide. He is using it as a symbol of spiritual transcendence. It is a symbol for the determination to be true to one's roots. Elesin's tragic flaw is his materialistic self-interest. Olunde's sacrifice symbolises a value higher than that of self-interest, and the external threat of an imposed alien culture. This ritual sacrifice is to be viewed as a willing sacrifice of an individual self on behalf of a religious principle. This action takes place at colonial Oyo during World War II and it is this colonial contact which determines the decision taken by Olunde. His sacrifice is an assertion of spiritual and cultural freedom. He rejects the Western education he has had, and the interference by the Pilkings. He wants to die of his own choice. He must spill his blood to redeem his father's unworthy character. It is not just the colonial factor that is in the foreground. The play depicts the psychological struggle of the main character with his beliefs, not the constraints imposed on him. A temporary weakness of will brings shame on him—he wonders if he is fated to destroy the society. Death as an act of will affirms his identity and destiny. Will is at the heart of Soyinka's vision. Tragedy results from the will of the hero to challenge the world. Hence, the play exemplifies the theme of his vision—a vision based on the African sense of communal well-being.

The ritual sacrifice forms the main motif of the play, Elesin is defeated by "a weight of longing on my earth-held limbs" (207). The reluctance of Elesin is a familiar psychological element in such a ritual. The enforced sacrifice is introduced in a context to stress the European ignorance. Pilkings deals with it as the sacrifice of a slave. His role is ambiguous—he is a colonialist who is satirised. His statements evoke such concepts as "human rights" and "freedom of conscience." When Elesin was to kill himself, Pilkings would have preferred not to interfere, but his position as a colonial functionary compels him to interfere.

> If they want to throw themselves off the top of a cliff or poison themselves for the sake of some barbaric custom what is that to me? If it were ritual murder or something like that I'd be duty-

> bound to do something. I can't keep an eye on all potential suicides in this province. (171)

Pilkings believes in freedom of conscience and sovereignty over his or her own body. A richly organic Yoruba universe has no place for individual rights. Elesin has not made a freely willed decision to accept a sacrificial religion. He has not behaved like a European stoic believing that a particular individual life is not worth living. Elesin Alafin means King's Horseman, and it carries with it the implication of his sacrificial function. His duty is to accompany the master to the other world; if he fails to do so, then the cohesion of the society will be ruined. The question of individual will exercising its power does not arise at all. The communal totality of "the living, the dead and the unborn" embraces the whole concept of individual will and the concept of individual volition becomes totally irrelevant.

Death here is neither barbaric nor civilized. Elesin exercises his will and commits the suicide. The tragedy lies in Elesin's 'laggard' will. He had been preparing for a different kind of death, and here death comes to him when it has lost its initial purpose. Soyinka neither approves nor disapproves of the act, but only unfolds the cultural sensibility. Elesin's death is purely a suicide without its original significance of the rite. The strength of will is seen in Elesin's dance, which is a kind of willed withdrawal from the life-force. He withdraws from it and as an act of will steps into the beyond.

Soyinka depicts a Yoruba society with its Africanist myth of simplicity, and its capacity to generate great euphoria in a cooperative society. All Yoruba characters accept the necessity for such a sacrifice. The Christian Joseph and Moslem Amusa are presented as *cultural mongrels*: they are horrified by Elesin's impious and selfish concern for his own individual survival. Dramatically effective is the assertion of a pure imaginatively rich, communal African totalitarianism against a hollow European, secular pluralist individualism. As Jeyifo complains, "In the process of polarising the conflict between an alien and an indigenous world-view, Soyinka has suppressed the real, objective differences between conflicting groups and classes within the indigenous system" (35).

A study of the social history of the country reveals a broad-minded spectrum of attitudes towards human sacrifice. Some divisions of the Yoruba society had a series of legal enactments clamped down on the practice of this ritual sacrifice. There are many instances where this ritual murder or sacrifice has been abolished. Soyinka's theme is thus to be seen in the perspective of the "voluntary" suicide of a vigorous adult male. The victim seems to accept the decision with a free will. To emphasise his theme, Soyinka presents him as a virile, dominant, socially prestigious man who is willing to offer himself for the sacrifice. Death seems to be induced by an act of metaphysical will. As Joseph remarks: "He will not kill anybody and no one will kill him. He will simply die" (167). Soyinka, it appears, has depicted the extinction of individuality at the behest of a totalitarian commercialism, but has given it an appearance of individual control and personal choice.

The personal dilemma of Elesin, who is cast in the mode of a tragic hero, forms the focus of our attention. It is evident that Elesin is dear to Soyinka's heart. In his search for a clear and dramatic metaphor for "the universe of the Yoruba mind" Soyinka has been confused. He has mixed up the primitive human sacrifice with a true African sacrifice of self. Olunde has not carved a niche in the playwright's heart. He is just a character created for ideological commitment but it is no substitute for genuine feelings. Soyinka draws a parallel between the forces at work in the colonial 1946 and the postcolonial 1974. The King of Oyo has died and the tradition is that the horseman Elesin Oba has to die in order to accompany him on his journey to the world of the ancestors. It is the eve of Elesin's death and the atmosphere is charged with excitement and expectation, such as is appropriate for any religious event. As it is his last day, he cannot be denied anything, not even bride.

The English Prince of Wales is to visit the town and the District Officer Mr. Pilkings does not want any untoward incident to spoil the smooth arrangements he has made for the Prince of Wales' visit. A ritual suicide by a major figure in the local hierarchy would jeopardise his chances of promotion. Hence, he decides to intervene, and arrests Elesin. Olunde, Elesin's son away in England for pursuing studies comes to pay his last respects to his father. The failure of his father to die is spiritually and socially disruptive, and Olunde takes his father's place.

A skeleton of a synopsis does not bring out the complexity of the plot. One must know something of the cosmology fundamental to the play. The essence of the Yoruba cosmology is in direct contradiction to the Christian and European emphasis on the individual, and the individual salvation. For the Yoruba, the emphasis is on the community, and the community makes no distinction between the living, the dead and the unborn. Soyinka visualises a fourth stage, a transitional phase. Elesin is about to undergo a transition—he is transition itself. Iyaloja gives sanction to the marriage of Elesin Oba and the young girl with the hope that any child born of the woman should be "neither of this world nor of the next. Nor of the one behind us. As if the timelessness of the ancestor world and the unborn have joined spirits to wring an issue of the elusive being of passage . . . Elesin!" (162). Elesin is both the mediator between the dead and the living, as well as the mediation itself.

The fulcrum of Soyinka's vision is will. The tragedy is a result of the Will offering a challenge to the world. Such determination marks his life too—his courage in defying governments, his survival after two years of imprisonment, his political involvement and his continuing creativity. Soyinka's work and life celebrate the human spirit. He aims at establishing a unity of personality in which art, religion and society coalesce. He adopts the African myth to the present situation—Ogun becomes the god of roads and of telephone wires, and carries the electricity of Sango. The myth forms a part of an active, dynamic, liberating African cultural and political assertion.

Elesin is the kind of ritual quester one finds in the plays of Wole Soyinka. He is in line with characters like the Bale, Jero, Professor, Kongi, the Madman. He talks himself into the transgression of boundaries and the fracturing of taboo. He is obliged to make use of the 'unused seed.' He acquires a young bride in order to leave behind an offspring, conceived at a critical time, and offer it as a special gift to the living he is leaving behind. It would be a child of transition, neither of this world nor of the next. Yet the gift is dubious, as it is an abiku, a half-child, which according to Yoruba belief is a miraculous monstrosity, a destroyer of mothers and a symbol of cultural and political deformity. Elesin's social position gave him the grasping appetite of a spoilt artistocrat: "The juiciest/Fruit on every tree was mine" (157).

"Not-I" bird folktale tells us the origin of death, and is an expression of the Yoruba world view in a capsule. Elesin creates dramatic vignettes of individuals' encounters with the 'death-bird.' It is like in Alarinjo masquerade. This is a popular form of dramatic entertainment (Alarinjo), which depicts through short episodes a wide variety of characters in stereotypical fashion. The natural, social and metaphysical world of the Yoruba is contained in Elesin's poems—all is controlled by and under the dominion of death.

> Death came calling
> Who does not know his rasp of reeds? (149)

Even Gods are fettered by their fear of death:

> Ah! companions of this living world
> What a thing this is, that even those
> We call immortal
> Should fear to die. (152)

Elesin, however, claims he is the master of his fate. "My soul is eager. I shall not turn aside" (153).

Elesin's heroism is that of the essential Yoruba man. The horseman's ritual is the transition of Elesin from the world of the living to that of the ancestors. The ritual drama is dissolving and reformulating the identification and fixing of the individual and social self. We understand that the ritual drama is a communal experience undertaken by the individual on behalf of the community. Strange voices guide Elesin's feet. In his Introduction to the play, Soyinka comments: "The confrontation in the play is largely metaphysical, contained in the human vehicle which is Elesin and the universe of the Yoruba mind—the world of the living, the dead and the unborn, and the numinous passage which links all: transition" (145). Elesin's will is polluted when the alien hand interferes. A strange force of violence shatters the mind's calm resolution, and he is prevented from committing the ritual suicide.

Much paraphernalia accompanies the man who is to make the journey to the other world. Elesin makes the final preparations to go from an earthly existence into the life beyond. He symbolises the transition, as his death is meant to make easy the passage to the life beyond. He is the symbol of a closing era. His fault is of the flesh. He is the link between his people and the spirit world of their late Oba. The impediment to the fulfilment of his mission comes in the form of his involvement with the maiden. A drumming sound is heard in the distance, and Mrs. Pilkings wonders what its significance is. Joseph replies: "I am not sure. It sounds like the death of a great chief and then, it sounds like the wedding of a great chief. It really mix me up" (170). Elesin thinks that he has the choice with him to exercise his free will. Hence, he chooses the maiden, and suspends, for a moment, the spiritual and common will of the people. The tussle between spirit and flesh entraps him—he falls into the gap between words and action.

Colonial masters are represented by Pilkings and the Prince. War in the play, is a symbol of time and transition—a time in which a society is changed, physically and psychologically. By wearing an egungun costume, Pilkings is involved in the act of defilement. This is intended to edify the colonial tradition, since it is meant to edify the visiting Prince. The wearing of egungun is a symbol of transition in Yoruba land, and Pilkings is at the crossroads of time and cultures. He does not care to understand the interpretation of the death of Elesin as interpreted by Elesin and his society. Elesin's people are disturbed as the pace of their sacred history is disturbed. The basic fault in Elesin is that he enjoys the pleasures of the flesh.

The women tease Amusa as "the white man's eunuch" (174). The white man cannot wipe out the imprints of tradition on Olunde's mind, or for that matter, any of the native's mind. "Is it not the same ocean that washes this land and the white man's land? Tell your white man he can hide our son away as long as he likes. When the time comes for him, the same ocean will bring him back" (175). The girls are a symbol of continuity as we expect them to grow into motherhood. This continuity is not a blind perpetuation of tradition, but a process of change through refinement. They want Amusa, 'the eater of white leftovers' to leave the place immediately. Olunde, on the other hand, seems to be turning back the hands of the clock. He had the opportunity to measure time with whiteman's clock; but the oppressive nature of tradition brought him back to bury his father, and assume the title himself. He does not respect what he does not understand of other people's cultures. The white man has and does observe his own tradition, but Olunde is not impressed with it, as it is beyond his ken.

The Christian is not able to view the colonial culture and religion in the proper perspective. The ritual suicide is a kind of sacrifice for the welfare of the community. Every society has its own built-in reserves of protecting the interests of its people. Mrs. Pilkings is unable to understand this point. Olunde's action does not acquire the desired meaning as, a substitute is after all a substitute. More than any one else, it is Iyaloja who has reverence for tradition. She dare not refuse to prepare the maiden for Elesin knowing that the maiden is already betrothed to her son. She is not totally willing, and does not give her consent wholeheartedly.

Elesin Oba is a failure. The failure does not represent the collapse of a cosmology. This collapse conceals the affirmation; it is not so about a failure. Search for the self's authentic being is always suspect. No one can seek it. Actions alone are the manifestations of the authentic being. Elesin is endowed with courage that is associated with Ogun. He on behalf of his people, single-handed, had to join the dead King to prevent the destruction of his people. He is the victim of his own strength. His failure is both individual and representative. He is an embodiment of the culture of his people, and as such has a great responsibility. He is accused of dereliction of duty. "You have betrayed us" accuses Iyaloja (210). Elesin who has worked for the welfare of the people is cast off and rejected. The element of pathos demands he be forgiven but sentimentality has to be renounced. He is a dramatic creation with mythic proportions of the great literary figures.

> He has the grandeur, dignity and pathos of Oedipus; the questing anguish of Hamlet; the restless and aspiring soul of Peer Gynt; the arrogance of Nietzsche's superman; the sense of comedy, love of life, and sensual proclivities of Dionysus; and the pathetic, rationalizing weakness of Richard II. (Bowman 94)

As a leader he might have failed, but he is still a man and his body deserves the respect accorded to the bodies of men. "However sunk he was in debt he is no pauper's carrion abandoned on the road" (219).

Iyaloja asserts her faith in the unborn. Soyinka may be accused of patronising a form of romantic primitivism. The opposite is the case with Olunde, the character who embodies the play's contemporary and significant affirmation. He is neither primitive nor romantic. We expect him to accept the leftovers of an alien culture, but we are mistaken. He shows that once the essence of the culture is absorbed, no exposure to glittering eye-catching dross can undermine it. He has learned what is fundamental to his integrity and to the integrity of his people. Soyinka advises us to undertake a vigorous journey of self-discovery, which might involve crossing a number of obstacles. It will demand great, perhaps, the ultimate self-sacrifice, but it is rewarding.

The play is actually the 'ritual itself' and a celebration of Yoruba culture, and a sacramental activity. Could we say that it is a celebration of the importance of tradition, a Yoruba version of Nietzsche's 'God is Dead'? The English couple has no religious awe. Jane Pilkings and her husband do not respect any traditional wisdom. Olunde is a man whose experience of the world outside has helped him to form a deeper understanding of his heritage and his relation to it. He had escaped from his father's stifling clutches to England. Now he appears, having heard of the king's death and to pay his last respects to his father, whom he expects to find dead. Olunde's firm belief is that Elesin Oba should die to join the dead king. If this ritual is not carried out, the world would be "wrenched from its true course" or smashed "on the boulders of the great void." He undertakes the task of avoiding the catastrophe, when the father fails. His death is a significant and uncompromising affirmation of traditional cosmology.

The fourth area—the area of the transition—is really the area of stress of the human will. The movement of transition is the state of paralysis where action is impossible. Elesin is neither dead nor has the will-power to carry out his duty. The play dramatizes the interruption of the psyche and cultural harmony of traditional Oyo society. The Yoruba market has an immense symbolic value—it is a microcosm. The Major Oba is addressed as Alaiyelcowa (owner of the world and of life), and the minor Oba as Oloja (owner of the market). There is also a saying—the world is a market, heaven is home. The rich and colourful cloth available in the market symbolizes or is rather the equivalent of the honour and glory awaiting the people's messenger to the other world. Elesin lusts for an unknown girl whom he chanced to see in the market stalls. The spiritual world is spoken of in material terms. Man in any environment must eat before he can philosophise. Elesin's failure is due to his excessive love of the material world. He functions well in his institutionalised role as a scapegoat, but when the time for action comes, he is ruled by his trickster motives. He blames his failure of nerve on "the alien hand [which] pollutes the sources of will" (211). The difficulty of conforming arises out of the trickster trait in his personality. Esu, the Yoruba trickster god casts his spell over him who serves as an agent of continual change and readjustment. Esu was held responsible for change and was branded as the confuser of men and the god of fate. The concept of Esu was used as a threat of individualism to social order—a mythical reality. In the past, the reluctance of chiefs who are expected to accompany a dead Alafin had grave moral implications. The members of the offending official's lineage would strangle him rather than suffer the stain of ignominy. By the end of the nineteenth century, the situation had changed. Men who were not willing, were never forced to do so.

The Oyo period which provided the material for *Death and the King's Horseman* had become less demanding than what is emphasized in the play. This was perhaps because of the economic and social developments which accompanied colonial rule. In this play, Soyinka stresses the importance of honour for the well-being of man by emphasising the need for transcendence of material goals. Tradition exerts its power on the dramatists as the Yoruba dramatists are close to their ancestral society. The logic of tradition seems to be working smoothly, until the intervention of the District Officer. Elesin is reluctant but is enraged at the interference of the white officer. The play is an exploration of the predicament of a human being, like Elesin who is facing the metaphysical abyss, and is afraid of taking the plunge into the unknown. His resolve to perform the role for his people fails on the brink of the transitional gulf.

Soyinka is not celebrating the ritual—he has cast his dice against it.. He sympathises with Elesin's basic human instinct for survival rather than for death. He dramatizes here the human plight, man's fear before the gaping chasm. Olunde, the foreign-educated son of Elesin, takes the headlong plunge, only for the sake of honour. Soyinka seems to question the communal demand which expects a man to sacrifice his life for the sake of some unidentified communal benefit. The play dramatizes 'a ritualistic encounter' with Death. The suicide is to be enacted by a powerful act of will-power, without external stimulus. The colonial factor in the play is a catalytic factor. The historical incidents of that Oyo society are used as an outer shell, filled with Elesin's metaphysical encounter with Death. The past is used to question or even to taunt the present in terms of attitudes to death and the human ways of coping with the phenomenon.

The entire first half of the play seems to balance on the brink of the metaphysical abyss. Elesin is aided by three media of human expression—incantatory poetry, music and dance; but, all three means fail to lead him into the metaphysical gulf. His dance is a spiritual device which enables him to step into the beyond. He attempts to meet the king in the other world. Elesin's death by strangulating himself is a concretization of his spiritual death.

The call of one's tradition or of one's blood is always louder than the voice of education. Olunde, despite his western education, is driven to sacrifice his life. This need not be taken to mean that Soyinka is a blind upholder of tradition against the forces of individual will. Man in his keenness to acquire glory makes the traditional ritual a scapegoat. Soyinka is making a derisive comment on the self-styled traditionalists. Life-sustaining powers form the backbone of society. It is not a clash of cultures that confronts us. It is a weakening of the impact made by tradition. Elesin's desire to live overrides the call of tradition. It will never do to believe that the European powers have the mission to nullify the eternal order of the gods. It is just one escape route sought by the protagonist to appease the demands of his will. The wise people absorb the best parts of modern civilization. Thus they steer clear of any confusion. This will to walk on the path towards progress without rejecting the bond of tradition is a characteristic of Ogun's representatives among men. A true representative of Ogun in this play is Olunde. He is nourished by western education, but is an advocate of the traditional values. His concern is with the welfare of the society at large, not just the individuals.

The dead king sends his messages to the Horseman through the Praise Singer. The dead man, for instance, tells him: "If you get lost my dog will track/The hidden path to me" (183). Elesin answers: "The seven-way crossroads confuses/Only the stranger" (183). A true servant of Ogun will not be confused by the seven-fold nature of the god; only strangers will be confused by this. Elesin is a representative of God as he ventures to stride across the gulf that separates the living from the dead. Ogun, too, risks his life in the abyss of transition in order to bridge the gulf between man and gods. New ideas have to be absorbed and assimilated in order to give strength to the bulwark of tradition. Olunde does just that—he combines modernity with respect for the essence of tradition.

The arrogant, supercilious and well-armed British confronted a well-rooted social structure and a metaphysical system which they could neither understand nor appreciate. Soyinka is hardly interested in presenting a ridiculous view of the Western concepts—he is only interested in presenting a strong defence of the Yoruba world. He reveals to the Nigerian leadership certain ideals of leadership, responsibility and self-sacrifice. Olunde is selected as the symbol of all this. He sacrifices his life not for personal aggrandizement but to save people from the wrath of God. His act is one which is done with the interest of the community in mind.

Soyinka as a poet, delights in twilight zones—between night and day or death and life. These are areas of transition in which he explored certain basic facts about life and death. In *The Road* he has explored in depth the shrouded middle passage between death, fleshly dissolution and arrival in the other world. "He has not felt obliged to cast off traditional thinking and dress himself in the tattered remnants of alien philosophies" (Roscoe 50). He has retained the essence; his is not mere lip-service but an involvement in a tradition that is still alive. Ogun is the god of iron and steel; he was a hunter deity. He is the god of war, of mechanics, and wood carvers. A protector of orphans, he stands for a transcendental, humane but rigidly restorative justice. He is the essence of destruction and creativity. He is Soyinka's favourite god. In one of his poems, "Season," Soyinka writes: "Rust is ripeness, rust" (*Idanre and Other Poems* 45). Ripeness stands adjacent to decay. In harvest time, the fruit (the life) Ogun has brought to ripeness, is already dissolving into death (as rust). The seven-fold nature of Ogun is brought forth in *Idanre* by Soyinka. The protagonist is mentally and physically prepared for his disintegration. The tragic action in Yoruba drama stems from a knowledge of the protagonists' foray into this psychic abyss of the recharged energies.

Advocates of tradition seem to judge the play *Death and the King's Horseman* as a triumph of the forces of tradition against human will. This, does not appear to be a correct assessment of the play. Elesin is expected to follow the king to the other world. "Our world was never wrenched from its true course," says the praise-singer. (149) The ritual is an act of honour. 'Life is honour' for Elesin. "It ends when honour ends." (154) Elesin has been a hard-core traditionalist. Much against his will, his son has joined the Medical School in England, with the help of Pilkings. Could it be that Olunde sought an escape from the oppressive stranglehold of custom? Later developments, of course, belie this assumption. The common man's belief is that the tradition will survive in spite of the efforts of the white man to stifle the same. Olunde's return vindicates this belief.

Olunde believes his father is dead or rather in his mind, he is already dead. Pilkings is shocked, as Olunde's way of thinking has not been affected by western education. Elesin is indignant, as Pilkings has disrupted his line of duty. "Take your albino's hand from me you . . . " he rants (202). Olunde's outburst is characteristic of a strong traditionalist—"I have no father, eater of left-overs" (203). External forces exert a pressure to bring about a rupture of the traditional matrix. Elesin and other votaries of the native faith are confident enough to withstand the ravages of western thought. "Did you think it all out before, this plan to push our world from its course and sever the cord that links us to the great origin" (205). Elesin's firm belief is that his son will avenge his 'shame.' "His spirit will destroy you and yours" (205). He is repentant and his people are keen on seeing him fulfil his duties.

The tussle between the individual will and the forces of tradition ends on an ambiguous note. Olunde avenges his father's outrage, and gives up his life. Elesin, prompted by his wounded conscience, commits suicide. Elesin and Olunde are both men of strong will. Olunde, born in the traditional set-up and nurtured by western ideas is an orphan. "O you poor orphan, what have you come home to?" (202). Jane Pilkings' words sum up his position. Perhaps, this motivated him to commit suicide. One wonders if this is the position of many of Soyinka's protagonists—people who are stranded between two worlds—one still powerful, and the other spreading its tentacles in order to engulf the former.

Man actually struggles to transcend his psychic alienation. An artist achieves this with the help of his imagination. For the common man, it is a formidable task. The primal severance of men and gods is of significance. Soyinka believes like Wordsworth that the need of the hour is to marry our minds to the external universe. He believes in the restorative power of the mystical communion of the contemporary psyche with its cosmic environment. This is illustrated by the myth of Ogun's quest across the gulf of transition. The basic premise is that severance of human essence and cosmic oneness has created a deep impact on the human psyche. It needs an immense effort of the will to cross the abyss. "Ogun," for Soyinka, "is the embodiment of Will, and the will is the paradoxical truth of destructiveness and creativeness in acting man" (*Myth* 150). In the ritual drama of Soyinka, the dramatist's task is the marrying of the "essence-ideal" with "materiality" on behalf of the entire community. The ritual is a cleansing and recreative ceremony and an attempt at diminishing the gulf of transition, and thereby strengthening the communal psyche. The ritual actor tries to go beyond his consciousness to embrace the primal reality.

These two plays depict the basic conflict between the two protagonists: Man and Destiny or Will and Tradition. The only certainty in man's life is reduction to nothingness—Death is inescapable. Man's mortality cannot be denied, and Abiku is a symbol of this. He flouts the traditional Yoruba's struggle to preserve life:

> In vain your bangles cast
> Charmed circles at my feet
> I am Abiku, calling for the first
> And the repeated time.
>
> ("Abiku," *Idanre and Other Poems*)

Man's anguish at the thought of Death is deepened, as he is conscious of his losing battle with Destiny. The road is one avenue which leads to Death. The road is a monstrous man-eater, and man is a pilgrim who must travel.

Professor's quest for the Word ends in a fiasco. It is a quest for something which is intangible and lost in obscurity. The elusive character of Professor baffles us—he does not achieve success, in the sense, he dies while trying to extract the meaning of Death. Steeped in corruption, he seeks ways and means of pursuing his metaphysical quest. New truths have to be unravelled, but they should be enclosed within the framework of possibility. Pursuit of the impossible and a mighty obsession is indicative of man's unstable mind. Professor appears to be one such character. The whole pursuit acquires bizarre proportions with the introduction of Murano, a boy in half-dead, half-living state. Soyinka seems to ring a warning bell. It is a sacrilege to interfere with providential scheme of events. Professor tries to tamper with the sealed secret and meets with a disastrous end. The will in a misdirected endeavour is bound to be ruined. Professor's death is not a punishment: it is a natural outcome directed by divine dispensation. No one can conqúer Death. Failure to do so, should not be construed as defeat.

Elesin Oba, as we have seen, is distracted by material gains offered to him. Caught in this web, he tries to snap his ties with the tradition, which demands that he accompany the dead king to the other world. His will dictates to him to stay on in this world. Again, it is his will which prompts him to perform the ritual suicide. He feels guilty about his aberration, and makes amends for it. Olunde, too, is prompted by his will. The two plays, thus portray protagonists who have a strong will, but are in constant opposition with the social framework. They are normal human beings ruled by their will. Social interference and coercion may play a part in their life but it is their will which survives. Professor may not survive or succeed, but he leaves behind a message—to aspire for something within one's reach. We can only say with Soyinka:

> Time's slaves
> Eunuchs of will wait upon you;
> . . . We,
> All whose dreams of fire resolve in light
> Wait upon the old ancestor in pursuit
> Of truth, and to interpret dreams. (*A Shuttle in the Crypt* 21)

Works Cited

Gibbs, James. "Soyinka in Zimbabwe: A Question and Answer Session." *The Literary Half-Yearly* 28.2 (1987): 50-110.

Jeyifo, Biodun. *The Truthful Lie: Essays in a Sociology of African Drama*. London:

New Beacon Books, 1985.

Katrak, Ketu H. *Wole Soyinka and Modern Tragedy: A Study of Dramatic Theory and Practice*. New York: Greenwood Press, 1986.

Ogunba, Oyin. *The Movement of Transition: A Study of the Plays of Soyinka*. Ibadan: Ibadan University Press, 1975.

Peters, Jonathan A. *A Dance of Masks: Senghor, Achebe, Soyinka and African Cultural History*. Washington, D.C.: Three Continents Press, 1978.

Soyinka, Akinwande Oluwole. *Myth, Literature and the African World*. London: Cambridge University Press, 1976.

______. *A Shuttle in the Crypt*. London: Oxford University Press, 1972.

______. *Idanre and Other Poems*. London: Methuen, 1967.

______. *Collected Plays 1*. (*The Road, The Swamp Dwellers, The Strong Breed, A Dance of Forests, The Bacchae of Euripides*). London: Oxford University Press, 1973.

______. *Collected Plays 2*. (*The Lion and the Jewel, Kongi's Harvest, The Trials of Brother Jero, Jero's Metamorphosis, Madmen and Specialists*). London: Oxford University Press, 1974.

______. *Six Plays* (*The Trials of Brother Jero, Jero's Metamorphosis, Camwood on the Leaves, Death and the King's Horseman, Madmen and Specialists, Opera Wonyosi*). London: Methuen, 1984.